For Edda

- Table of Contents -

continued. . .

Table of Contents (continued)

Kenneth D. Alford

Nazi Plunder

Great Treasure Stories
of World War II

DA CAPO PRESS

A Member of the Perseus Books Group

Cataloging-in-Publication data for this book is available from the Library of Congress.

First Da Capo Press edition 2001
Originally published by Savas Publishing Company in 2001.
Originally published as *Great Treasure Stories of World War II.*
ISBN 0–306–81241–X

Published by Da Capo Press
A Member of the Perseus Books Group
http://www.dacapopress.com

Da Capo Press books are available at special discounts for bulk purchases in the U.S. by corporations, institutions, and other organizations. For more information, please contact the Special Markets Department at the Perseus Books Group, 11 Cambridge Center, Cambridge, MA 02142, or call (800) 255-1514 or (617) 252-5298, or e-mail j.mccrary@perseusbooks.com.

1 2 3 4 5 6 7 8 9—06 05 04 03

List of Photos and Illustrations

~ The photos and illustrations of the
treasures discussed in this book are found throughout its pages ~

Credits:

Preface

World War II—the cataclysmic event of the Twentieth Century—has been documented in fact and fiction by writers working in a variety of media. From great battles to fascinating personalities to the horrors of the concentration camps, the war of all wars has been covered on all fronts.

In the past few years, a growing number of authors have focused on the material plunder of the war in Europe: Most recently, Holocaust-era assets and reparations payments to survivors of Hitler's death camps have occupied the front pages of the world's newspapers. Ken Alford's *Great Treasure Stories of World War II* continues this fascinating investigation and offers incisive looks at not only the Nazi looting of German-occupied countries, but also American involvement in the looting of treasures our soldiers were entrusted to safeguard. This book provides eye-opening accounts of villains and heroes in these underhanded scenarios, proving all too clearly that once again where there is gold (and other riches) there is bound to be greed—even among normally upright, law-abiding men and women.

Great Treasure Stories of World War II makes for entertaining, illuminating reading and is popular history that touches upon the tragic, the loathsome, and at times, the comic, while at the same time meshing smoothly into the mainstream of World War II movements and events. It does not attempt to cover the subject completely (an impossible task in even the thickest of books) but, rather, through individual examples and tales of lust and greed and criminality, adds to our understanding of the atmosphere and motives of those last days of the greatest conflict.

It is engrossing reading, and a valuable contribution to our understanding about those dark days.

Larry C. Bush
Pensacola Junior College. Milton Campus

Introduction

World War II was the most devastating conflict in human history. The sheer scope of devastation wrought by the global conflict, coupled with the material loss and displacement of millions of people, was simply staggering. The nature of the aggressive war waged by Germany, which overran much of Europe and western Russia, led to the plundering of many countries. Germany's rapacious acquisition of valuables was not an aberration of human greed, but merely a continuation of the practice from previous secular and religious crusades during other periods of hostilities. What set apart the years 1939-1945 was its exceptional scale and well ordered ruthlessness.

Between September 1939 and May 1945, German armed forces roamed from Dunkirk to Stalingrad, and from Spitzbergen to Athens, plundering gold, silver, currency, paintings and other works of art, coins, religious artifacts, and millions of books and other documents. The value of these items, many of which were one-of-a-kind priceless pieces, can be estimated in billions of dollars. The artwork alone, for example, looted under Adolf Hitler's direction, exceeded the collections amassed by the Metropolitan Museum of Art in New York, the British Museum in London, the Louvre in Paris, and the Tretiaskov Gallery in Moscow.

After the end of the war, reparations for these cultural losses were demanded from Germany by a host of nations and individuals.

Until recently, American involvement in the acquisition of these treasures has largely remained obscure and misunderstood. The sad and embarrassing fact, however, is that many Americans participated in widespread theft in the weeks and months following the end of the war. Much of this activity was sanctioned by the United States government. In just the art domain alone, American soldiers snatched thousands of paintings, sculptures, and drawings, as well as tons of valuable photographs and negatives. Huge numbers of books, documents, and other manuscript collections, courtesy of the U.S. Army, reside today in the Library of Congress in Washington, D.C. American officials even authorized the removal of Europe's best horses to the New World.

Although Congress has passed legislation authorizing the return to Germany of much of this material—supported by federal court rulings—the large bulk of valuables carried to our shores remains in American archives and in private collections. There have been few if any real attempts to return the war booty. United States officials recently announced that two tons of Nazi gold is stored at the Federal Reserve Bank in New York City. This statement was released only after prodding by Senator Alfonse M. D'Amato during his investigation of the Nazi gold deposited in Swiss banks during World War II.

Recently, the *New York Times* and other distinguished periodicals have featured stories about Russian treasures taken from Germany during the closing days of the war. According to these articles, both the Hermitage Museum in St. Petersburg and the Pushkin Museum in Moscow hold immense numbers of paintings seized from the Germans, who had earlier plundered these items from other countries and private collections. The Russians were not the only ones engaged in this unseemly behavior. While Moscow was packing and shipping art and other items of value for its journey eastward, the United States was orchestrating its own version of postwar pillaging. Under the direction of U.S. Army officer Gordon Gilkey, for example, approximately 11,000 paintings were transported to Washington, D.C. in 1947, where they were placed in "permanent retention" in the Pentagon. The most valuable of these are today stored in an underground vault at the U.S. Center of Military History in our nation's capital. The official looters ranged from government officials to private individuals, many of whom went on to prominent positions in government and private industry.

One case of ransacking even involved former President Herbert Hoover. After the cessation of hostilities, Hoover toured the globe in President Harry Truman's airplane, affectionately named "Faithful Cow." Hoover's irreproachable objective during this trip was to address the threat of hunger by finding a method to feed the starving children of the world. While Hoover was on this noble mission, his staff was in Germany collecting thousands of articles for the Hoover War Library at Stanford University. One of the items taken was German Propaganda Minister Joseph Goebbels's 7,000-page typed diary. One of Hoover's aides, Frank E. Mason, negotiated a $400,000 agreement with Doubleday for a partial publication of the diary. The money might have been better used to help feed the starving children. *The Goebbels Diaries*, with an introduction by war correspondent Louis P. Lochner, was published in 1948. The original diary is still in the Hoover War Library at Stanford University.[1] In addition to Goebbels's diaries, the Hoover Institute acquired a collection of his personal papers dating from 1931 to 1945. The former president's agents also acquired large collections of paper items that once belonged to Heinrich Himmler and the Nazi Party; even manuscripts relating Aryan folklore ended up at Stanford University.

Numerous accounts have now surfaced establishing government-sanctioned plundering and an extensive disregard for cultural objects by individual soldiers and civilians. However well intentioned some officers and departments might have been, however, it was simply impossible to prevent widespread looting during the period of enormous disorder that followed World War II. Command and troop relocations made it impossible to effectively safeguard the many important museums and repositories sprinkled across Europe. German citizens, staggered by the consequences of war, could not protect the cultural objects in their homes, castles, and museums, from which they were often evicted by American military personnel. While acquiring the "spoils of war" may have been widespread and common, the fact remains that looting by U.S. troops was illegal. Certainly some soldiers were ignorant of this fact, but many others knowingly and willingly grabbed what they could, tempted by the glitter of so much priceless treasure strewn about them.

The plight of these celebrated works of art and other vanished treasures during the closing days of World War II is a remarkable tale of greed, lust, fraud, deceit, and treachery. Much of this story is found in *Great Treasure Stories of World War II*.

And so much is still waiting to be written.

Acknowledgments

I am grateful to the many people and institutions who helped with the research and writing of this book. It could never have been completed without their assistance. I know I am missing someone, but you know who you are and my thanks are everlasting.

Special thanks are due to the following individuals: Klaus Goldmann, Berlin, Germany; Willi Korte, Germany and Silver Springs, Maryland; John Toland, Danbury, Connecticut; Larry Bush, Pensacola, Florida; U.S. Army Judiciary, Falls Church, Virginia; Mary B. Dennis, Deputy Clerk of Court, Archives and Record Services, Washington D.C.; John Taylor; Richard Boylan; Rebecca Collier; David Giordano; Vickie Washington.

I would also like to extend my appreciation to Birch Lane Press for permission to use material from my earlier book, *Spoils of World War II*. Thomas M. Johnson allowed me to use information from his book, *World War II German War Booty*.

I would like to offer special thanks to my publisher, Theodore P. Savas, for his added knowledge, editing, advice, and encouragement during this project. I am grateful for his support and direction.

Last but not least, I pay tribute to my wife Edda for her patience during the research and writing of this book. Without that support, the task I undertook would have proved impossible.

Chapter One

The Allied Capture of Nazi Gold

In 1933, Adolf Hitler became Chancellor of Germany. It had been a long and arduous climb to power. The son of a civil servant and future Führer of the Third Reich was born in Austria in 1889. After failing to acquire a seat in the Vienna Fine Arts and Academy in 1907 and again in 1908, Hitler spent time in Vienna until the outbreak of World War I, when he joined the army and was sent to the Western Front. He served honorably and bravely throughout the war, was wounded twice, and awarded the Iron Cross, First Class. The defeat of Germany in 1918 devastated Hitler, who thereafter aligned himself with the right-wing radicals of the German Worker's Party—the genesis of the Nazi Party.

By 1924, Hitler had emerged from a stint in prison for his radical activities and began transforming the National Socialist German Worker's Party (NSDAP) into a national organization. It garnered some six million votes and seated 107 members in the Reichstag in the 1930 elections. Seeing the future, industrialists and others with political interests and money began donating to Hitler's party. By 1933, Hitler and his associates scored an impressive 52 percent of the vote. Now, as Chancellor of Germany, Hitler moved quickly to solidify his power and revive the German military and war industry. With anti-Semitism as the keystone of politics, he transformed the Nazi party into a tyrannical mass movement.

The Führer of Germany carried out his plans with breathtaking speed. Within six years he had moved troops into the Rhineland (a violation of the Versailles Treaty), altered the terms of a naval treaty with Great Britain, annexed Austria, and occupied the Sudetenland. The Germany army, or Wehrmacht, and air force, or Luftwaffe, swelled in size and strength. Perhaps most ominously, Hitler executed a non-aggression treaty with the Soviet Union, which freed Hitler to operate elsewhere in Europe without having to worry about the Bolshevik menace to the east.

Hitler invaded Poland in September 1939, triggering World War II well ahead of his own schedule when Great Britain, followed by France, declared war on Germany. The Poles were quickly overpowered, but the British and French allies offered little more than threatening words in response. In the spring of 1940, Hitler's forces overran Denmark and Norway, and a few weeks later marched into the Netherlands, Belgium—and France. The Battle of Britain followed, and although it was a close affair, Hitler was unable to force an English capitulation. Driven by a hatred of Bolshevism, Hitler turned his attention to his erstwhile ally, the Soviet Union. The massive June 1941 invasion carried the victorious German armies to the suburbs of Moscow, but stout Russian opposition and an early winter stopped Hitler's panzers and foot soldiers shy of the decisive victory they were seeking. While Hitler's troops were freezing and dying in Russia, the Japanese sallied out and struck the United States at Pearl Harbor on December 7, 1941. In perhaps his most serious strategic blunder, Hitler declared war on America, ensuring Yankee support for embattled Britain and the Soviet Union.

Thereafter, Germany's fortunes took a decided turn for the worse. An entire German Army was gobbled up at Stalingrad on the Eastern Front, and Field Marshal Erwin Rommel's Afrika Korps was defeated in North Africa. German cities felt the routine sting of bombs dropped by American, Canadian, and English planes. Equally devastating was the loss of the critically important Battle of the Atlantic—Hitler's attempt to cut off supplies flowing to and from his allies with his vaunted U-boats. By the time the Allies invaded France at Normandy on June 6, 1944, it was obvious that Germany could not win the war. Less than one year later, with the Russians fighting in the streets of Berlin, Hitler killed himself in his bunker on April 30, 1945, along with his long-time mistress Eva Braun, whom he had married one day earlier.

History's most devastating war was over. Tens of millions of soldiers and civilians were dead, millions more were displaced, and Europe's Jewish population had been largely wiped out in the "Final Solution." In addition to this human devastation, Hitler's attempt to dominate and control Europe and the Soviet Union had resulted in the Nazi confiscation of much of Europe's priceless artwork, precious metals, jewels, and other valuables.

*   *   *

In early 1945, three million Allied soldiers smashed the Siegfried line and broke into Hitler's "Inner Fortress"—Germany. During this massive offensive, General George Patton's Third Army dashed through Thuringia Province and discovered the largest single cache of treasure of World War II.

Located within the Kaiseroda Mine at the village of Merkers in Thuringia was the most valuable prize of World War II—the main cache of Germany's gold reserves removed from Berlin because of Allied bombing. In addition, millions of Reichsmarks, U.S. dollars, and other paper money had found its way to Merkers during the early months of 1945.

After the capture of Merkers, the Allies began hearing rumors of recent movements of gold from the German Reichsbank in Berlin to the Kaiseroda Mine. The rumors persisted, but no eyewitnesses were located until the morning of April 6, 1945. Two military policemen, Privates Clyde Harmon and Anthony Kline, stopped two displaced French women from Thionville who were violating an order prohibiting civilians from moving around the 90th Division command post at Keiselbach. One of the women was pregnant and was being accompanied by her friend in a search of medical assistance. After questioning by the military police at their headquarters, the women returned the two miles to Merkers, accompanied by an army private.

When he got to Merkers, the private saw the large buildings and the tops of the elevator lifts at the Kaiseroda Mine. A simple inquiry into the nature of the facility prompted the women to reveal that the mine was where the Germans had deposited their gold reserves and valuable property of the National Art Museum of Berlin. The gold, they continued, was stored 1,600 feet deep, and local civilians and displaced persons had been pressed into service unloading and storing it and currency as well. They did not know the quantity or value of the cache, but it took a crew of

The entrances to the Kaiseroda Mine were covered by several large, five-story brick buildings housing electrical coal-fired generators. These generators produced electricity for lights, ventilation fans, and power for the large elevators used in the mineshafts.

men three days to unload and store it. The stunned private reported this conversation to Lieutenant Colonel William A. Russell, Military Government Officer for the 90th Infantry Division. Russell proceeded immediately to the Kaiseroda mine and interviewed displaced persons living in the area. The remarkable story as relayed by the French women was true.

Realizing the importance of this discovery, and with the war still raging in Germany, Lieutenant Colonel Russell requested the 712th Tank Battalion to proceed to Merkers to guard the mine entrance. The mine, Russell soon learned, was honeycombed with 35 miles of tunnels and boasted five entrances. The entire U.S. 357th Infantry Regiment was dispatched to guard it. Within days, the Kaiseroda mine was secured by reinforced rifle companies, antiaircraft guns, tanks, tank destroyers, and jeeps mounted with .50-caliber machine guns.

On Saturday, April 7, members of the 80th Division decided to examine the contents of the tunnels. After entering the mine, Lieutenant Colonel Russell made several attempts to open the vault door with a set of keys. Unsuccessful, Russell tried to knock down the door with brute force, which simply resulted in shearing off the door handles. Frustrated, Russell suggested digging through the masonry vault wall, but it was determined that blasting an entrance in the vault wall the following morning would be easier. Russell and his party moved on to examine an extensive collection of art found in various tunnels. The next day, a Sunday, Russell and General Herbert L. Earnest, Commander of the 90th Division, reentered the Kaiseroda Mine. This time Russell's efforts would not be denied: accompanying him were men of the First Battalion, 357th Combat Engineers.

The engineers at first attempted to dig a hole through the masonry vault wall, quickly discovered the barrier impregnable to shovels and picks. Explosive charges were set. While the men sat on stacks of currency stored outside the vault, the explosives detonated, blasting an entrance approximately four by eight feet. The vault itself was 75' by 150', with a 12' ceiling. Although well lighted, it was not ventilated. What the men saw astonished them: they had just uncovered 285 tons of gold bars and gold coins, and $519,805,802 in cash.[1]

In the Versailles Palace outside Paris on Sunday, April 8, 1945, Colonel Bernard Bernstein, who was on General Eisenhower's SHAEF

The treasure recovered by the U.S. Army was stacked in long single rows with a two-and-a-half-foot separation between the rows of bagged gold coins and bars. Hundreds of valises, heaped in the back of the vault, contained gold and silver jewelry, priceless church ornaments, table and silverware, and bales of currency. A narrow-gauge railroad track ran through the center of the vault.

staff, was enjoying a late breakfast at the officers' mess before heading over to his office with a copy of the military newspaper *Stars and Stripes* tucked under his arm. Before starting work, Bernstein glanced at the front-page and saw the story about American troops and the gold cache stored in a salt mine at Merkers, Germany. Shortly thereafter, Bernstein's telephone rang. It was General Frank J. McSherry from SHAEF's headquarters at Rheims, France. General George Patton, McSherry explained, had asked General Eisenhower to take over the responsibility of handling and safeguarding the Merkers treasure. That afternoon Bernstein was on a small plane flying to Rheims to help arrange the

Bags of gold coins were opened and examined. In order to examine the contents of the bags, the Americans had to break open the seals. At one point, a bag of gold coins was opened and poured into a steel helmet, photographed, and returned to the bag. Each bag of gold coins weighed 81 pounds.

takeover of the treasure in the name of the commanding general, European Theater of Operations, United States Army.

One of Bernstein's tasks was to find a suitable place to store the gold, art, and currency. He decided the Reichsbank building in Frankfort would be an excellent repository. That same day, April 10, Colonel Bernstein drove the 85 miles to Merkers and reported to the 357th Infantry Regiment. After making a preliminary inspection of the Kaiseroda Mine and its contents, he left instructions with the officers to call his hand-picked men and assign them the task of auditing the valuables in the mine.

The indefatigable colonel next traveled to Patton's Third Army command post, located near Merkers, to explain to the general that the valuables must be moved to Frankfurt as quickly as possible. Patton, however, opposed the idea. "There is no chance the Germans can push me out of this area," explained the general. "It is safe to leave the gold and other treasures down in that mine."

Bernstein, however, did not back down. "I don't for a minute question the correctness of your statement, but under the Big Three arrangement, this part of Germany will be taken over by the Russians after the fighting ends and we certainly want to get all of this out of here before the Russians get here."

Patton was astonished by Bernstein's statement. "I didn't know that at all," he said, "but I will do everything possible to facilitate your mission."[2] At this stage of the war, it seems incredible that Patton was not aware of the four-zone division of Germany by the Allies.

Colonel Bernard Bernstein, the Director of the U.S. Military Government Finance Division, being awarded a French military decoration.

On April 11, Bernstein set up a command post in Merkers. The necessary office equipment, mess, billeting and other facilities were brought forward to the area. Bernstein wasted little time getting down into the mine for a look around. Years later he explained, "Because of my background with the Treasury Department and working for a large law firm that provided attorneys for the old Farmers Loan and Trust Company in New York, the first thing you do is, you want to know what you have got. Make sure that you are accounting for it properly."[3] His inspection included the examination of a number of art treasures from the Berlin Museums, with Dr. Paul W. Rave, Curator of the Berlin Museum, present to furnish information concerning the pieces. A number of cases were sitting in a pool of water, and Bernstein arranged for these to be moved to higher ground within the chamber. When he returned to his quarters that night, a message from General Patton was waiting for him. It instructed Bernstein to be at the entrance of the mine the following morning at 9:00 a.m.

Colonel Bernstein and his staff were at the mine long before the appointed hour to continue the inventory. At 9:00 a.m., the colonel took the elevator up to the entrance, but no one had yet arrived. Suddenly, the front end of a jeep bearing a plaque with five gold stars in a circle drove up the entrance. Colonel Bernstein automatically straightened up. He knew there was only one person entitled to that designation in this theater. As he offered a crisp salute, he found himself looking into the faces of General Dwight D. Eisenhower, General George Patton, and General Omar N. Bradley—the three highest-ranking American officers in Europe, all in one jeep.

General Manton S. Eddy joined the group as they approached the elevator to descend into the mine. The elevator that would carry them into the mine was suspended by cables within a 1,600-foot shaft. Colonel

Generals George Patton (left), Dwight Eisenhower (examining chest), and Omar Bradley (right) inspect the main vault. A dark shadow was cast over their exhilarating find when it was discovered that 207 boxes and valises contained thousands of gold and silver dental crowns, bridges, plates, silver tableware, watch cases, eyeglasses, gold wedding rings, pearls, precious stones, and assorted currency—the economic remnants of Nazi atrocities.

Bernstein, however, had not been informed that he would be meeting a collection of the top-ranking generals that morning. As a result, he had not replaced the German elevator operator. Standing on the wooden elevator platform, Bernstein reflected to himself: "We were fourteen stars and just a colonel in the hands of a German who could have really upset the whole plan at that point. If that German running the elevator had been a fanatic, you never know what might have happened."[4] Fortunately, the operator guided the group safely into the mine. As they stepped out of the elevator at the bottom of the shaft, the U.S. Army guard saluted the top brass and was heard by all to mutter, "Jesus Christ."

The generals looked at the artwork, which was later ascertained to constitute about 25 percent of the contents of the vast Berlin Art Museums. They also examined the plates used by the Reichsbank for printing currency. As they made their way through other tunnels, Colonel

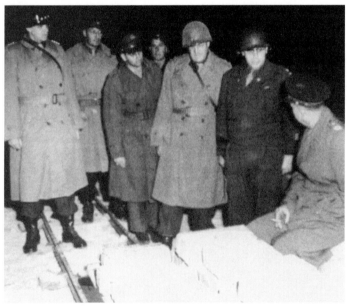

General Eisenhower was particularly interested in learning about the contents of the mine. He sat on a large stack of currency smoking a cigarette as Bernstein told the generals about the gold, currency, and valises filled with loot from concentration camp victims. General Eisenhower looked through a number of valises; one ladies' small traveling bag still had the fresh aroma of perfume inside.

General Eisenhower (front), with Generals Patton (center) and Bradley (left), examining pieces of art that Patton later described as "the type normally seen in bars in America."

Bernstein explained the plan for the inventory and removal of the treasure from the Kaiseroda Mine. The tour lasted over an hour. At one point Eisenhower noticed some writing on the wall. It was in German, and he asked Bernstein to translate. Although Bernstein didn't know German, he knew enough Yiddish to read it: "The state is everything and the individual is nothing." "What an appalling doctrine," Eisenhower's reply.

Patton was not impressed by the artwork. He later wrote in his diary, "The ones I saw were worth, in my opinion, about $2.50, and were of the type normally seen in bars in America."[5] The general was referring to hundreds of the world's greatest paintings.

On the afternoon of April 12, 1945, Bernstein telephoned Captain Henry Morgenthau III, the son of the secretary of the treasury and a member of Patton's staff. Bernstein wanted to discuss with him the treasure found at Merkers, but Morgenthau was not available. Bernstein retired for the evening around midnight, but a short time later a soldier entered and informed him that Captain Morgenthau had returned his call. The voice on the phone shook Bernstein wide awake. "I suppose you are calling me about what you heard over the radio," asked Morgenthau. When Bernstein replied that he had not been listening to the radio, Morgenthau interrupted him: "President Roosevelt died." Bernstein remembers hanging up and returning to bed. Unable to fall asleep, he spent the night tossing and turning, lamenting the president's death.[6]

On April 14, ten days after the Kaiseroda Mine discovery, the treasure was ready to be removed. The first of the two elevator shafts was designated to lift currency and other miscellaneous items to the surface. Shaft two (which broke down and was repaired by engineers stationed nearby) was earmarked to haul the gold. Thirty ten-ton trucks pulled up to the mine at 7:30 a.m. Large tarpaulins were spread out in the back of each, and after they were loaded, folded over to conceal the gold from view. Security was doubled around the salt mine.

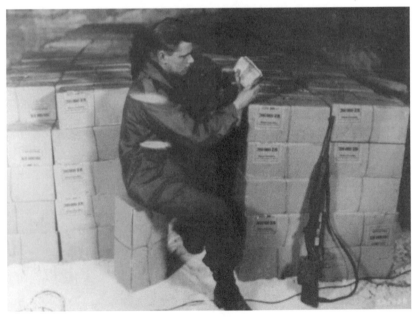

An American soldier counting Reichsmarks currency.

During 1945 the Foreign Exchange Depository, located in the Reichsbank building in Frankfurt, accepted 78 shipments of gold and had stored in its spacious vaults 387,536 pounds of gold bars and 313,411 pounds of gold coins. Colonel Bernstein (hatless, right) and members of his staff examine gold bars stored in one of the 18 separate compartments inside that facility.

Loading continued throughout the night. Each truck was filled over capacity to carry the huge load away. As the laborious process dragged on, the drivers and assistants took the opportunity to grab some sleep in the cabs. The loading was finally completed at 7:45 a.m. Three of the trucks were jammed with artwork; the remaining 27 contained gold and currency. Bernstein was understandably nervous about the safety of the shipment. First, he insisted that a military guard ride up front with the two drivers. Still not satisfied with the arrangements, he asked Lieutenant Colonel John H. Mason, commander of the 357th Infantry Regiment, to post one of his soldiers on the back of each truck to prevent the possibility of German citizens jumping on board and stealing some of the gold or currency. "I think we can take our chances with the Germans," explained Mason. "These are very tough soldiers."[7] He was right. With all the roads and intersections blocked to other traffic along the 85-mile route to Frankfurt, the convoy made it to the Reichsbank at 3:45 p.m. without incident.

The guards stationed at the Reichsbank were reinforced by the soldiers accompanying the convoy. Eight M8 tanks and ten antiaircraft guns were added to the existing security already in place. Now, over 700 combat troops were guarding the Merkers gold. Unloading began immediately with the help of 150 U.S. Army Engineers, and continued throughout the night and into the next day. The U.S. Army had seized 235 tons of treasure from the designated Russian occupation zone—the largest gold appropriation in military history. This constituted only the first deposit—569,726 pounds of gold—made to the "Allied Gold Pot." The Reichsbank was surrounded with barbed wire placed under constant surveillance by guards in watchtowers. At night, floodlights illuminated the building.

General Walter Bedell Smith, Eisenhower's chief of staff, asked Colonel Bernstein to furnish him with five gold coins to make medals for

An American soldier stands guard as a two-and-a-half ton truck is loaded with gold to be returned to France. This gold would greatly aid France in overcoming her post-war financial difficulties.

Dutch gold consisting of 209 boxes of gold bars and 223 boxes of gold coins is being loaded into trucks provided by the Dutch Army. Colonel Van Limberg, general inspector of the Netherlands Army, and his dog, were in command of the move.

President Harry Truman, Prime Minister Churchill, General Marshall, Field Marshall Montgomery, and General Eisenhower. The request took Bernstein by surprise. The army and the American government, he replied, had a fiduciary responsibility for the gold. General Eisenhower might be subject to criticism for taking gold coins, he added. The colonel was trying, as diplomatically as possible, to tell the general "no." Not to be denied, General Smith asked General McSherry to ride with him from the supreme headquarters building to the Reichsbank; he would get the coins himself. As they were driving toward the bank, McSherry advised Smith that Colonel Bernstein had set up tight security around the building, and that it was unlikely they would be allowed to enter. Disgusted, Smith ordered his driver to turn around and return to headquarters.[8]

Bernstein's concern for the safety of the shipment proved well founded. Although he had done everything he could, $12,470 in U.S. currency disappeared from the Merkers mine. During the transfer from Merkers to the Reichsbank in Frankfurt, a large number of Dutch gold coins and 468,800 Reichsmarks ($46,880) were also stolen. In spite of an investigation by the commanding officer, European Civil Affairs Currency Section, the currency and gold coins were never recovered.[9]

The bulk of gold seized by the U.S. Army and stored in the Reichbank at Frankfurt was eventually distributed to various Allied nations. After the transfers were completed, 108,952 pounds of gold (1947 value $45,759,840) remained in Allied Gold Pot. This author filed a civil action suit to attempt to obtain information as to the final disposition of the remaining gold. These records, however, are still classified "Secret" under FOIA Exemption (b) (1), and Presidential Executive Order 12356. Former Senator Alfonse M. D'Amato (R-NY) recently addressed the fate of the gold during his investigation of wartime Swiss bank and Nazi gold transactions. (See Appendix A for the author's spreadsheet analysis of German gold activity.)

In addition to the Kaiseroda mine, there were dozens of other mines in the immediate area containing over 800 miles of tunnels that were also examined for hidden treasure. One of the more interesting was the Ransbach salt mine. The main chamber of the mine was 2,500 feet below the surface. Inside was an estimated two million books from the Berlin Library. The first shipment of books arrived in the middle of 1944. By 1945, 200 loaded railroad cars of books had been jammed into the mine. The volumes were primarily reference and reading books, categorized as old, rare, or valuable. Some contained reference maps, others theatrical and operatic manuscripts, and musical scores from the State Theater. In addition to the books, the mine held 45 cases of art containing approximately 500 paintings of international reputation and high value. The mine also housed 200,000 theatrical costumes hanging from long poles suspended from the ceiling.[10]

The surface building and elevator of the Ransbach salt mine.

Chapter Two

The Plundering of Munich

On May 1, 1945, after completion of the initial phase of the battle for Munich by the U.S. 3rd Infantry Division, the city was assigned to the highly secretive Task Force (T Force) of the Sixth Army Group. T Force had been organized in the early stages of the war to recover German technology, including patents and blueprints for heat-seeking missiles, jet aircraft, rockets, and other modern weapons of mass destruction.

T Force targets included the *Führerbau*, and the *Verwaltungsbau* (Administrative Building). These twin buildings served as headquarters for the Nazi Party and were located on the reconstructed Königsplatz. To the rear of the Führerbau was an older building known as the *Braunes Haus,* the birthplace of the Nazi Party. The structure had served as the original Nazi Party headquarters until the party grew too large to be housed within its walls. These three large buildings were connected by a vast system of tunnels complete with underground kitchens, dining rooms, communications centers, and storerooms. The complex contained vast quantities of Nazi memorabilia and was described by an army captain as "so goddamn much you could never go through it unless you made it a definite target to exploit at great length."[1]

By war's end the Braunes Haus, or at least that portion above ground, had been destroyed, but the other two buildings were largely undamaged

Due to the complexity of the Königsplatz, members of T Force
obtained this postcard and wrote in the locations of the buildings.

except for broken windows. Considerable looting by the retreating
German army had already taken place by the time American forces
captured these buildings. Papers, personal effects, photographs, and a
large collection of miscellaneous items were found scattered on the
floors.

The 1269th Combat Engineer Battalion followed the 3rd Infantry
Division into Munich, and was also assigned to T Force. The 1269th was
responsible for blowing open any safes found in the captured complex.
The engineers also strung communications wire from the buildings to the
T Force Command Post, and served as guards in and about the network of
structures. The men of the 1269th had no idea just how fortunate their
new posting would prove to be: the tunnels honeycombing the
three-building complex were crammed with valuable paintings, party
records, silverware, and many other valuable items gathered by the Nazi
Party.

In addition to the 1269th Combat Engineer Battalion, various units of
the 45th Infantry Division and 163rd Combat Engineer Battalion also
jointly guarded the buildings. Pvt. Theodore J. Polski and Pvt. John A.
Fraser walked into the Führerbau and discovered several enlisted men,
together with officers from the 45th Infantry Division, pocketing
silverware for souvenirs. The guard on duty at the time did not seem to
care, and two more captains, a pair of colonels, and a nurse corps WAC

captain joined the growing group of souvenir hunters. Polski joined in, picking out a set of silverware. Each piece had the initials "A.H." and a swastika. Fraser took eight sets of knives, forks and spoons. During the excitement of removing this vast collection of silverware, soldiers from the 1269th loaded several trucks with large quantities of silverware and other souvenirs.

Both Polski and Fraser returned to the their headquarters and showed their booty to their commanding officer, Captain Sterling F. McKee. The privates carefully wrapped their silver in a box and had Captain McKee write "Censored by Captain McKee" on the outside of the packages. Polski mailed the 80-piece set of silverware to his wife in St. Paul, Minnesota, while Fraser also mailed his booty home.[2]

This is how the basement of the Verwaltungsbau (Administrative Building) looked when the U.S. Military Government took over its control.

In the waterlogged basement of Führerbau, an unidentified American sergeant was rummaging through the heaps of paper and personal items when he discovered a box. Inside were some of Adolf Hitler's most personal belongings, including his gold plated pistol. The container also housed Hitler's swastika ring, a tiny oil painted portrait of his mother, a framed photo of his German Shephard, Blondi, the swastika blood flag belonging to the unit of a comrade killed in the Munich Putsch of 1923, and numerous pieces of silverware with the initials A.H. These items turned up in a private collection in 1981.

The lucrative looting of the Führerbau, the Verwaltungsbau, and the Braunes Haus continued unabated until June 10, when the complex was taken over by a military detachment. The Property Control Officer ordered the complex ringed with barbed wire and guard stations. This put a stop to the pillaging by German civilians, but American soldiers and displaced persons climbed through windows and helped themselves to a wide array of valuable souvenirs.

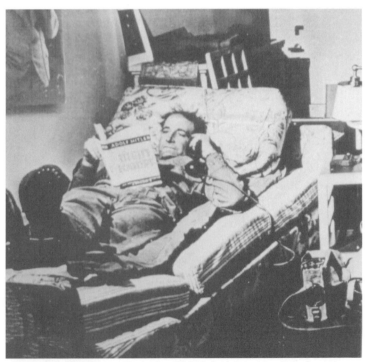

Sergeant Arthur Peters relaxing on Hitler's bed. Peters took the lamp (seen on the small table in the upper right hand portion of the photo) home. After his death his wife sold the lamp to a private collector.

Flag and China taken from the Führerbau or Party Headquarters in Munich.

Hitler's gold pistol (above) was valued at more than a million dollars. It was donated to the West Point Museum, where it can be seen today.

(Right): Hitler and his beloved dog, Blondi.

(Above) Hitler's silver tea service.

(Below) Linen with his initials A. H.

Chapter Three

Hermann Göring's Art Treasures

ermann Wilhelm Göring was born in 1893 at Rosenheim in Bavaria. After attending the Karlsruhe Military Academy (1905) and then the cadet school at Lichterfelde (1909), he was commissioned a lieutenant in the 112th Infantry in 1912. Thereafter Göring transferred to the air service. He carved out an impressive career as a fighter pilot and squadron commander during World War I, during which he was painfully wounded. In the early 1920s, during the turbulent aftermath of the Great War, he met Adolf Hitler and joined the nascent Nazi party. His close ties with Hitler guaranteed him a place in the new government Hitler was planning to instill in Germany. In 1935, two years after Hitler became Chancellor, Göring was appointed *Reichsminister* for Air and commander of the Luftwaffe. It was a job to which he was well suited; in just a few short years, Göring organized and built the world's best air force.

Unfortunately, Göring's strategic ability was not on a par with his organizational competence. His sharp opening act in Poland and during the early days of the invasion of France pleased Hitler, but his planes failed to stop the Dunkirk evacuation and the Führer began losing confidence in him. Göring compounded his mistakes during the Battle of Britain. Instead of continuing his successful attacks against the RAF

Hermann Wilhelm Göring. His Pour Le Merite, or Blue Max, hangs from his neck in this pre-World War II photo.

planes sitting on the ground, he changed course and launched massive air raids against English cities. As a result, he failed to destroy the RAF and earned Hitler's wrath in return.

The Führer turned his back on Göring for good after he failed to resupply the embattled German Sixth Army on the Eastern Front at Stalingrad, something he had promised Hitler he could accomplish. As the final days of the war played out, Göring offered to replace Hitler, who was trapped in his bunker in Berlin. The furious German leader dismissed him and accused the fallen Reichsmarschall of treason. Only the end of the war saved him (and perhaps his family) from a German firing squad.

In addition to his inept handling of the Luftwaffe, Göring was an avid collector of art. His interest, however, was purely personal and not historical. Göring began to collect art objects in a modest way after World War I. By the time the Nazi Party rose to power in 1933, he and Hitler had formulated a plan for Göring to gather a large art collection that would eventually be presented for posterity to the Third Reich. These art

One of the grand halls inside Göring's Carinhall estate, built on a rolling expanse of forest and lakes two hours' drive northeast of Berlin.

treasures, plundered from almost every country in Europe, were eventually housed at Göring's palatial estate, Carinhall, named after Göring's first wife, Baroness Carin von Kantzow of Sweden, who died in 1931. It was Göring's fervent desire that the home would someday be transformed into a tourist mecca, with its own special rail line straight from Berlin.

The stone and concrete Carinhall was constructed in the center of a hunting preserve—in addition to being an official thief, Göring was also an avid hunter—near Schorfheide, two hours northeast of Berlin. Its seemingly endless series of ballrooms, dining halls, libraries, and passageways were jammed with cultural objects looted from the finest collections in Europe. A magnificent domed library held a desk of mahogany twenty-six feet long, complete with inlaid bronze swastikas. The library also boasted a pornographic table supported by four large legs replicated to resemble penises, each inserted between a pair of female breasts. On the lawns of Carinhall were carved French Cupids, Greek satyrs, busts of Roman matrons, alabaster vases, Renaissance sun dials, and tons of weathered antiques and classical garden trimmings.

The head of Germany's Luftwaffe often used implied threats to get others to gather valuable art for him and his beloved Carinhall. Alois Miedl, for example, was a Dutch art dealer and banker who had moved to Holland from Munich in 1932. He had known Göring for a number of years, and thus the Reichsmarschall appreciated Miedl's Achilles' Heel: his wife was Jewish. Göring shrewdly offered protection for Miedl's

(Left) Alois Miedl, his Jewish wife, and their two children.

(Above) Rubens's *Diana at the Bath*, a $600,000 painting (1945 value) was acquired by Hermann Göring. (Below) Dozens of masterpieces graced the halls of Carinhall. These photos and others like them were used by U.S. officials to identify Göring's possessions at Carinhall. The photos are now in the Library of Congress.

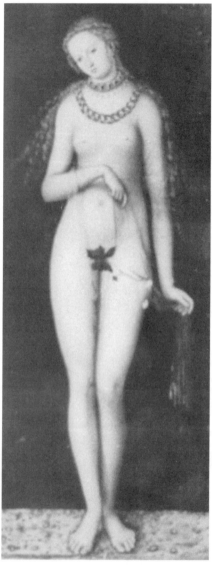

Göring had an absolute obsession with the works of Lucas Cranach (1472-1553). Cranach exhibited an intense interest in landscapes and in the expressionistic possibilities of the human figure, including this florid nude *Venus*, types of art especially prized by the Reichsmarschall.

wife. Miedl, in turn, had little choice but to scour Holland on Göring's behalf, buying and looting numerous priceless artworks, including the vast and well-known Goudstikker Collection. Miedl was not the only agent employed by Göring. The former World War I ace had stretched his tentacles throughout occupied Europe through a number of persons and organizations. The Reichsmarschall later insisted he always paid for his art, but payment was usually in the form of worthless paper currency or in exchange for other items. Sometimes he overpaid for art in his mad frenzy to acquire a desired piece. Still, it was an arrangement that suited Göring perfectly, and his wealth, as a result, increased by leaps and bounds.

Göring liked to refer to himself as a "renaissance man," and he consciously worked to develop this public persona. The business of collecting art grew to an obsession with him, and dominated every phase of his life. Indeed, the collecting passion even interfered with his military

Göring's train was adorned with velvet upholstery, rich tapestries, wood paneling, oversized bathtubs, tiled bathrooms, large double-bed sleeping rooms—and attached flatcars bristling with antiaircraft guns.

duties. The fact that Göring saw this vast collection as his legacy only drove him to buy and steal more. By the beginning of World War II in 1939, his collection numbered about 200 of the world's finest pieces. By the end of the war, he "owned" 1,375 paintings, 250 sculptures, 108 tapestries, 200 pieces of period furniture, 60 Persian and French rugs, 75 stained glass windows, and 175 other miscellaneous objects of art. There is little doubt that Göring's boast was accurate: he indeed possessed the most valuable art collection in the world.[1]

By January 1945, however, it was obvious even to Göring that he would not be enjoying his collection for much longer. As the Russians approached Carinhall, the Reichsmarschall decided it was time to remove his art collection and other personal belongings to southern Germany. Göring toured Carinhall with Walter Hofer, director of the official Hermann Göring Art Collection, pointing out what he wanted transported and what he wanted left behind. The artwork and other valuables selected by Göring were carefully packed in crates padded with straw, loaded onto Luftwaffe trucks, and sent to the local train station. During this process many large valuables were buried on the grounds of the vast estate. The most famous of these was a marble statue of Venus given to Göring by the Italian government. When questioned about these actions later, Göring admitted, "There was a great deal of stuff buried there. Also, the Russians will not let you dig there." After concealing the valuables, the German

30

soldiers Göring employed for the task were dispatched immediately to the Russian front.

Under the command of Fritz Görnnert, Göring's art train was packed with food, large pieces of antique furniture, large paintings, Gramophone records, and Göring's library, consisting of 240 linear feet of books. As the train was traveling in the direction of Berchtesgaden, Göring received disturbing news that the large underground command center in Obersalzberg had not been completed. As a result, the train's valuables were transported directly to Neuhaus, a town near Nuremberg, where they were unloaded

Göring dining room (top) and bedroom (above) at Veldenstein, his 16th century castle. Göring's spent time here in his youth. His mother was the mistress of owner Hermann Epenstein, who spent more than $300,000 renovating the castle. Even during the later stages of the war Göring was continuing the restoration, using more than 100 Italian artisans and spending a million gold marks a year.

onto local trucks and stored in Veldenstein castle, a 16th century structure inherited by Göring from his young stepmother, Lily von Epenstein.

In early April, another of Göring's trains loaded, containing by far the most important part of Göring's collection from Carinhall, was ordered to Berlin. The train also contained furniture and rugs, as well as the personal luggage of Emmy Göring, who had complained that not enough of her belongings had been packed onto the train. The cars remained in Berlin for several days before beginning the journey to Berchtesgaden.

Göring's problems were just beginning. On April 7, 1945, the Allies approached Veldenstein. Faced with a similar situation he had only narrowly avoided with the Russians, Göring again ordered all the castle's art treasures removed. The valuables were packed into eight freight cars, and a few items of value from the castle were added to the original shipment. Large quantities of clothes, soap, liquor, and personal luggage were also piled onto the train, which left Neuhaus on April 10 and arrived at a siding near Berchtesgaden the following night around midnight. There, the *Flitzer*, Göring's special "fast train" from Berlin, joined it.

At Berchtesgaden, Göring's found four trains at his disposal. It is incredible that at this point in the war that Göring could still find four trains to transport his personal property. The German army was retreating on all fronts in utter chaos. Wounded German soldiers were everywhere. Some were trying to save themselves on horse-pulled wagons. Others, the unlucky ones, remained lying in the mud and snow, dying a slow death where they had fallen because there was not any means of transporting them to safety. In the midst of all this suffering, Göring had commandeered two primary and two secondary trains in full operation for the pleasure of his personal entourage.

Some 14,000 freight cars arrived in Berchtesgaden during the war's final weeks. The heavy rail traffic was the result of a buildup centered around Berchtesgaden, where work proceeded at a frenzied pace in anticipation of establishing Hitler's headquarters outside Berlin. Thousands of laborers had worked day and night for a month building fortifications, as weapons, ammunition, and food rolled in as fast as the railroad marshaling yards could handle them. In the midst of this confusion Göring arrived with his trainloads of prized loot.

One of Göring's three train cars at Berchtesgaden. These, and five others at Unterstein were plundered and wrecked by the local population, the 3rd Infantry Division, the Free French, and 101st Airborne Division.

As his collection was being unloaded in Berchtesgaden, Göring, in a most uncharacteristic role, removed a picture and gave it to Christa Gormanns, his private nurse since 1933. As he handed her Vermeer's *Christ and the Woman Taken in Adultery*, Göring remarked that the sale of the painting would support Gormanns and her family indefinitely. Gormanns left the train with the large unframed painting in her possession.

Emmy Göring left the train carrying four small *Angel Musicians* paintings by Hans Memling. The Memling pictures were originally painted on both sides of a single piece of wood. They were split in two and thus became four paintings after Göring acquired them. The Reichsmarschall left the train with the *Rothschild* and *Renders* Memlings, a Roger van der Weyden, a French primitive, and his personal jewelry. Göring and his wife had removed six Memling angels from the vast collection. Since three of these six valuable paintings later disappeared, there is considerable confusion as to which paintings were stolen after being taken into custody by U.S. troops.

The American army continued advancing into Germany. Unwilling to surrender, Göring and his staff fled Obersalzberg for Mauterndorf castle, located 150 miles away in the southeast corner of Austria. Göring had inherited the Austrian castle, but had never lived there. Instead, he had given it to his sisters. As Göring was leaving Berchtesgaden for Mauterndorf, his staff began unloading the treasure from the trains. Most of the contents were stored in the Stabsamt, an unfinished underground command post situated along the road from Berchtesgaden to nearby Königsee. The valuables were stored in a tunnel on the third underground level. The entrance was sealed with concrete.

By the time French and American troops approached Berchtesgaden on May 4, only about one-half of Göring's collection had been safely stored away. In an effort to keep the valuable cargo away from the Allies, the Germans sent five freight cars to nearby Unterstein just a short stop down the line, while three other cars containing furniture, Göring's library, and art records remained at the main station in Berchtesgaden. French armored divisions opened fire on the three Berchtesgaden freight cars, ripping apart numerous paintings with machine gun bullets, and destroying a number of sculptures.

It was plain to everyone that the war was quickly drawing to an end. The following day, much of the population of Unterstein was gathered at the small rail station, fighting its way into the freight cars and carrying away booty, cutting up large carpets, and beating and scratching each other in their greed to obtain a part of Göring's "heritage." Several women cut an 18th century French rug into four pieces. It was still so large that several of the women subdivided one of the quarters into three separate sections. In this manner paintings, rugs, gold coins, and other valuables, as well as sugar, cigarettes, coffee, and expensive liquors found their way into the homes of the people of Unterstein. These valuables were hidden in homes, barns, woodsheds, haystacks, and even under manure piles. Göring's valuable collection of liquor—which had arrived on several cars four weeks earlier— was also popular with the civilians. As the locals raided the liquor, their drunkenness only added to the chaos. When questioned later about the brazen looting, several admitted that they were too drunk to remember what had taken place.[2]

Members of the 101st Airborne eventually moved into the area around Berchtesgaden and assumed control of the situation. Before long it became obvious that Göring's vast art collection had been dumped into their lap. After some intelligence gathering, Captain Harry V. Anderson, of Ossining, New York, suspected that the Stabsamt, the unfinished

Members of the 101st Airborne Division at the entrance of the Stabsamt, an underground chamber containing a vast amount of Göring's treasure. The American Soldiers called this concrete hideaway "Aladdin's Cave."

underground command post, might have a side room off the tunnel. A sounding device was used to explore the chambers and a hollow area was soon located. Unwilling to use explosives, the soldiers began chipping away at the entrance. It took three days of hard work to break through eighteen inches of cement into Göring's treasure room. What was left of

the art collection sat alone in the damp darkness—not exactly the Hermann Göring had envisioned. It took three days to remove all of the valuables from "Aladdin's Cave."

Captain Harry Anderson collected all the art he could find in Göring's abandoned three railroad cars at Berchtesgaden and five at Unterstein. The photo on the opposite page shows the priceless *Madonna with Child* being carefully unloaded.

The American soldiers did not hesitate dipping into this large pool of valuables. Layton F. Jones discovered a locked trunk in the Stabsamt at Berchtesgaden. Jones forced the case open and removed a silver-bound copy of *Mein Kampf*. This valuable book was number 33 of only 100 handmade volumes made to commemorate the printing of the one-millionth edition of Hitler's memoir. The book was later sold to a private collector.[3]

One member of the 101st Airborne found Hermann Göring's Carinhall guest book, bound in solid silver, inside "Aladdin's Cave." The first page contains the note: "With the most cordial wishes for happiness and bliss," and was signed "Adolf Hitler, Berlin April 10, 1935." The book contains the signatures of many distinguished guests, including American President Herbert Hoover. General Maxwell Taylor donated the volume to the West Point Military Academy Museum in 1948.

Captain Harry Anderson (right), with an unidentified American officer admiring Hermann Göring's favorite painting, Vermeer's *Christ and the Woman Taken in Adultery*. Anderson seized the artwork from Christa Gormanns, Göring's private nurse, who was given the painting by the Reichsmarschall himself. Unbeknownst to any of them, the painting was a fake.

Göring's Carinhall guest book, bound in solid silver, was found inside "Aladdin's Cave." The first page contains the note: "With the most cordial wishes for happiness and bliss," and was signed "Adolf Hitler, Berlin April 10, 1935."

Göring's treasures were stored in a guarded and fireproof three-story rest center for rail workers in Unterstein. Military collector Mike Morris, who lives in San Antonio, Texas, owns the sign in the above photo. He has offered to sell it for $25,000.

Items in this room are solid gold and worth millions of dollars. In the center foreground is a gold sword presented to Göring by Italian leader Benito Mussolini.

Captain Anderson was only to happy to commandeer Göring's favorite painting, Vermeer's *Christ and the Woman Taken in Adultery,* from its new owner Christa Gormanns, Göring's private nurse. Anderson and others were unaware that origins of the painting were in some doubt. In August 1945, Hans Van Meegeren, a painter of some talent, was arrested by the Dutch

American soldiers admire some of the sculptures acquired by Göring.

Göring's paintings alone (above, opposite page) filled 40 rooms! Four rooms and a wide corridor were jammed with sculptures. Other rooms (below) were piled high with tapestries, and barrels and boxes of porcelain and silverware.

authorities for his collaboration with the Nazis. Specifically, he was charged with allowing *Christ and the Woman Taken in Adultery* to be sold to Hermann Göring. The defense offered by Van Meegeren stunned the Dutch: the artwork was a fake! Since no one believed him, the forger offered to

One of the rooms under the protective custody of the 101st Airborne. The white figure on the left is Luca della Robbia's *Mary Magdalene and the Urn*. In the center are Pisan's *Madonna* and *Angel of Renunciation*.

complete a "Vermeer" (*Christ Among the Doctors*, also known as *Young Christ*) to prove his claim. He was locked away in a room with several witnesses and guards, and two months later completed the work. The paintings were indeed forgeries, a bombshell that rocked the art world.

How had all this come about? Shortly before the outbreak of World War II, previously unknown Vermeers were "discovered." Unknown to anyone at that time, these magnificent pieces were the work of Van Meegeren. His goal was to embarrass Europe's art critics, who had described his own work as worthless and his abilities as minimal. The seven fake paintings earned Van Meegeren $3,024,000 from the most prestigious art museums and collectors in Europe. The artist was sentenced to one year in prison, but died soon thereafter before completing his term.

Only one day before he committed suicide in Nuremberg, Göring was gleefully informed by the Americans that his precious Vermeer was a fake. Did the fallen Reichsmarschall already know this? Perhaps that explains why he has given it to the unsuspecting Fräuline Gormanns.

– Chapter Four –

The Capture of Hermann Göring

On the evening of May 7, 1945, German Corps G, First German
Army, and the U.S. Seventh Army negotiated a cease-fire.
During this time Reichsmarschall Hermann Göring sent a note to
Seventh Army Headquarters in Kitzbühel, Austria, informing the
Americans that he would meet them and surrender at Fischhorn Castle at
Zell am See. At this time Göring was staying at his Mauterndorf Castle,
about 100 miles from Fischhorn. Germany surrendered the next day, May
8, and General Robert L. Stack, assistant division commander of the U.S.
36th Infantry Division, traveled to the castle with a platoon from the
636th Tank Destroyer Battalion to accept Göring's surrender.

When Stack and his men arrived at the castle, they found it occupied
by armed troops of the Waffen SS *Florian Geyer* Division. This rather
unsettling situation continued for three hours while members of the SS
tried to locate Göring. Stack was eventually informed that the former
commander of the once-vaunted Luftwaffe had been held up because of
German roadblocks and snow on the roads.

Determined to reach Göring, General Stack, his aide Lieutenant
Harold Bond, and a German major, climbed into a jeep and staff car and
drove to find him. One can only imagine the surprise of the German
troops when an American army general, a first lieutenant, and German
major drove through German roadblocks seventy miles behind German

Hermann Göring after his capture by members of the 36th
Infantry Division. The look on his face indicates that he has
at least an inkling of what is in store for him.

lines in search of Hermann Göring. Regardless of the danger, Stack
wanted the glory of capturing the highest ranking surviving Nazi. He was
no more than 30 miles from the Mauterndorf Castle when he found the
Reichsmarschall and members of his household stopped along a country
road a few miles from Radstadt. Stack and Göring got out of their
respective cars, walked towards each other, and saluted. Stack asked
Göring if he spoke English. Göring said no, but that he understood it
fairly well. Stack informed him that he had received his letter and would
accept his surrender immediately and take him to Fischhorn Castle at Zell
am See. The Reichsmarschall was to be sent to Seventh Army
Headquarters either that night or the next day. Göring's remarkable life
was about to enter its final phase.

It was about 8:30 p.m. on May 8, 1945, when Stack and his men
turned around and headed back to Fischhorn Castle. No difficulty was

encountered passing through the German roadblocks or entering the American lines at St. Johann, and the entourage arrived at Fischhorn Castle around midnight. They were 20 miles from Kitzbühel and Stack decided to spend the night there. Göring's staff was ordered to deliver any arms they possessed to Stack's room. The order horrified Göring, who promptly explained that the SS troops might kill him, since Hitler had ordered his arrest and execution prior to committing suicide in his underground Berlin bunker. Stack modified his directive and allowed four members of Göring's staff to keep their pistols and sleep in the front part of the room occupied by the Reichsmarschall.

Once situated, Stack notified the commander of the 36th Division, General John E. Dahlquist, that Göring was under arrest. The following morning Stack had the SS troops disarmed and at about 10:00 a.m. left in his staff car, followed by Göring, for the trip to Kitzbühel. Göring was taken to the division command post at the Grand Hotel, where he was introduced to Dahlquist. After exchanging salutes, the two officers talked briefly about the size and location of Göring's staff. Generals Dahlquist, Stack, and Walter W. Hess, along with Göring, shared a drink and then ate chicken, peas, and mashed potatoes for lunch, as it was "fried chicken day" for the entire staff.[1]

At this point Göring asked for an interview with General Dwight D. Eisenhower. In addition to other matters, it was the Reichsmarschall's hope that the general would place Göring's family under the protective

Göring insisted upon a bath and fresh uniform before he would pose before this 36th Division flag at Fischhorn Castle. Military awards were never worn on an overcoat. Was Göring shrewdly playing to his captors by attaching his Pour le Merite (Blue Max) and other medals and posing in front of his conqueror's flag? His medals were later stolen.

Göring with Major General John E. Dahlquist, commander of the 36th Infantry Division, and Brigadier General Robert C. Stack on the balcony of the Grand Hotel in Kitzbühel, Austria, shortly after Göring's capture.

custody of the U.S. Army. According to Göring, the interview would be a conversation on a human and soldierly level. Dahlquist telephoned Göring's request to Seventh Army Headquarters, which in turn contacted Eisenhower. The response must have dismayed Göring: Eisenhower probably would never talk to him, and he would be treated like any other captured German general.

The release of photographs of General Dahlquist and Göring to the press elicited a negative response from the American public at large. Charges of fraternization with the enemy were thrown about, and angry denunciations were written and mailed to Dahlquist. One letter read as follows:

> Sir,
>
> I have 2 sons who were <u>killed</u> by <u>Goering</u> over there. You have discrased [sic] our <u>U.S. Army</u> uniform.
> Why don't you resign the Army and stay over there and suck the hind tit of Goering??
> Answer this in the public press, if you dar—if you don't will follow this up in the press.

Reichsmarschall Hermann Göring at the Seventh Army headquarters. His Field Marshal's baton can be seen in his left hand, rolled up in green felt cloth.

Although many citizens later believed Göring enjoyed preferential treatment in the hands of the Americans, he certainly did not think so. Instead of a hearty welcome by the supreme Allied commander, the Reichsmarschall was stuffed into a small two-seater liaison plane, a Stinson L-5 Sentinal. General Walter Hess and Colonel Bernt von Brauchitsch, Göring's assistant, were loaded into two Piper Cubs and flown to Augsburg, Germany, the location of the U.S. Seventh Army Headquarters and Interrogation Center. The faster 130 m.p.h. L-5 arrived first and waited thirty minutes for the Piper Cubs. There was no one to meet the party because ground transportation had been dispatched to the wrong airfield. An hour later, the men were picked up by a staff car and driven to Seventh Army headquarters.

On the afternoon of May 9, word spread throughout Seventh Army headquarters that Reichsmarschall Göring had arrived. The former head of the once-vaunted Luftwaffe swaggered into the Seventh Army Interrogation Center carrying his Field Marshal's baton rolled in a green

Göring was relieved of his military medals, including his Grand Cross, Pilot-Observers Badge with diamonds (above) and his dagger (below), all while being forced to sit in a small straight back chair designed for a man half his girth. He was obviously ill at ease and sweated profusely throughout the ordeal. In the background stands Colonel Bernt von Brauchitsch, who is removing his own medals.

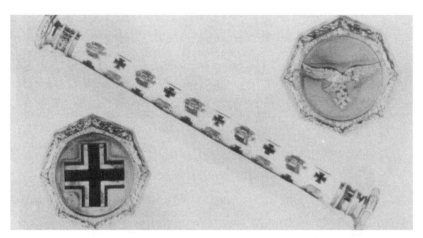

This field marshal baton was taken from Göring when he surrendered to the U.S. Seventh Army on May 9, 1945, and was presented to General Alexander M. Patch. A swastika with inlaid diamonds crowns the top of the baton.

felt cloth, adorned with his best medals, a unique hunting knife, and a pistol.

The Seventh Army commander, General Alexander M. Patch, was at the command post of XV Corps when Göring arrived, so he was taken to Patch's second in command, General Arthur White. Göring entered, and White motioned him into a chair. White politely asked Göring about his family and assured him no harm would befall them and that they would be kept under American guard. Göring replied with a dignified head bow and an audible "thank you." White's line of questioning covered several areas, including the whereabouts of Hitler and the former commander of the SS, Reichsführer Heinrich Himmler. Hitler was certainly dead, Göring replied. He was less sure about Himmler's fate, although the last information he had placed him near the border of Denmark. White informed Göring that he would be housed in whatever means were available to an army in the field. White rose, his nod indicating the interview was over. Göring rose, clicked his heels, raised his baton in a salute, and did not wait long for a return salute that never came.

As Göring was taken away, White informed Colonel William W. Quinn that Göring's baton was the badge of office of a Field Marshal, just as a sword or saber is the badge of an officer of lesser grade. Quinn was instructed to seize the baton from Göring. When General Patch returned,

Göring's Field Marshal's Baton. When General Patch returned to the U.S. in June 1945, he presented the baton to President Harry Truman, who kept it on his desk for awhile before returning it to General Patch. The 56-year-old Patch was assigned commanding general of the Fourth Army, Fort Sam Houston, Texas, until his untimely death from pneumonia on November 21, 1945. On March 23, 1946, Göring's baton and dagger were placed in the West Point Military Museum. The baton is valued at $1,000,000.

the baton was presented to him as a token of surrender from the man who had once identified himself as Hitler's successor.[2]

In 1963 the Department of Defense wrote General (former Colonel) William W. Quinn and Major Paul Kubala letters requesting information on the whereabouts of Göring's medals. "I doubt they can be recovered, for the simple reason that on the occasion of his surrender they were not considered to be of any interest," was Quinn's rather odd reply. According to Kubala, Göring "was in possession of all his medals and decorations" when he departed.

Robert Kropp, Göring's personal valet since 1933, traveled by car and arrived that night at Seventh Army headquarters. Kropp immediately met with Göring and was introduced to the camp commander, whom he later described as a "U.S. Colonel" of German extraction who spoke German with a Berlin accent. In the evenings, usually after 6:00 p.m., the camp interpreter would come by and take Göring to the colonel's house, where the two would sit and drink until 2:00 or 3:00 the next morning. Göring would return in a fairly intoxicated state. It was not unusual for him to visit the colonel during the day

This American revolver (left) and dagger (below left) were worn by Reichsmarschall Göring and taken from him when he was captured. The revolver, a .38 caliber Smith & Wesson, was in the possession of General Arthur White until 1958. A runic inscription on the hilt of the dagger (an ancient Scandinavian alphabet) translates: "From Eric to Hermann." Eric was Count Eric von Rosen of Sweden, the brother of Göring's first wife, Karin. Both items are on display today at the West Point Military Museum.

and sit out in the garden. On one of these festive occasions, Göring told the colonel that he had a painting worth $400,000 (1945 value) and that he was willing to give it to the colonel as a present. Göring informed Kropp that the colonel had migrated to America as recently as 1928, and that he was the son of a Prussian security police master musician of the so called "Mai-Kaefers (May-Bugs)."

On May 10, 1945, after spending a day with Göring, interrogator Major Paul Kubala wrote a detailed report about the encounter.

"Although he has been depicted in news reports as being half-mad," explained the major, "Göring gives the impression of being a highly intelligent and cunning man, with charming manners and certain knowledge of art. He is very talkative, and once he has started to develop a favorite theme he can hardly be stopped. According to the report, Göring "explains his tremendous accumulation of treasures by claiming to be a great lover of artistic works, and by stating it was his intention to transform Carinhall (his residence) into a national museum. 'After all, I'm a Renaissance type.' explained Göring.[3]

On May 15, after five days of interrogating Göring, Major Kubala telephoned Colonel Quinn, informing him the former Reichsmarschall had access to a famous painting. If he were allowed to collect some clothes from Fischhorn Castle, explained Kubala, Göring would turn the painting over to the military authorities. Kubala asked if he could send one of his men to collect the art. Quinn instructed his subordinate to type a note addressed to Frau Göring over the Reichsmarschall's signature, instructing her to turn the painting over to Kubala, together with shirts, underwear, and Göring's best uniform—the Bismarck Rock, a uniform of the Old Prussian Political Party.

The following day the officer and the valet Kropp returned to Augsburg with the clothing, a photograph of Emmy and Edda Göring in a silver frame, an accordion, and a Memling masterpiece wrapped in a towel, the small 6-by-10 inch (15-by-20-cm.) *Madonna with Child.*[4]

Kubala took the painting to Colonel Quinn, and the two men

Madonna With Child. The 6 x 10 inch Memling was never recovered. Today, this painting is estimated to be worth some $250 million.

carried it to General Patch's office. Patch was not in, so Quinn dismissed Kubala and left the valuable painting on the general's desk. Quinn called the headquarter's photographer to come over and shoot the priceless art. Several people, including James J. Rorimer and Major John Jack H. Smith, gathered to admire the Memling. Rorimer cautioned Quinn to advise the photographer to handle it with the utmost care. Upon reflection, Quinn decided not to have the painting photographed. Numerous people passed in and out of Patch's office, and the $400,000 Memling vanished.

On May 20, 1945, Göring was transferred from Seventh Army headquarters to the Grand Hotel in Mandorf-les-Bans, Luxembourg. Much to the Reichsmarschall's displeasure, his new accommodations were anything but "grand." In fact, his small unlit room on the fourth floor was utterly spartan in every respect. His circumstances substantially worsened when, on August 12, 1945, he was sent to his final destination: Nuremberg and solitary confinement. During a round of questioning, Göring complained to his American interrogator, Herbert Steward Leonard, that "every item has been taken from me including the smallest items that my little daughter received as baptismal presents. Everything has been taken from me except a hat, a dress, a blouse, two shirts, and one pair of shoes. Everything has been confiscated from my wife. I merely wish to state this because it is being denied here [by the Allied powers]." [5]

Emmy Göring's circumstances were considerably better than her husband's. After Hermann Göring was captured, Frau Göring remained at Fischhorn until June 11, 1945, when she left for her large estate at Veldenstein Castle. On that same day Göring's Mercedes and a German truck with an attached trailer were loaded with the goods that Göring had brought with him from Mauterndorf Castle on the day of his surrender.

Frau Göring's party was provided with a U.S. military escort under the command of a lieutenant with the 101st Airborne Division. During the 200-mile trip, the trailer overturned and the goods were reloaded onto an American truck. These items included French champagne, Puerto Rican rum, and 40 cartons of cigarettes. The arrival of this escorted convoy gave the local population at Veldenstein Castle the impression that Frau Göring was a royal subject of the American conquerors. Emmy Göring and her staff moved into the spacious and comfortable living quarters, where they were joined by a resident cook and handyman. Frau

Frau Göring at Fischhorn Castle, recovering from a heart attack she suffered after the arrest of her husband.

Göring's maid later explained that her duties included bathing and dressing Frau Göring.

This cosy arrangement did not set well with Lieutenant Hubert J. Tyrrell of the 90th Infantry Division, who was present when the entourage arrived. The following day Tyrrell had the Mercedes confiscated, and a day later had two military members of Frau Göring's staff taken to a prisoner of war internment center.

After Frau Göring's return to Veldenstein Castle, members of the 90th Division were instructed to search the castle for weapons and other

Hermann Göring's Veldenstein Castle.

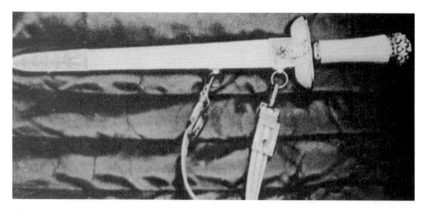

Hermann Göring's Reichsmarschall Dagger, described as the Mona Lisa of daggers.

contraband, a commonplace practice at the end of the war. The company commander, Major Orvin C. Talbot, issued orders that an officer must be present in each room to guarantee that no looting took place. A day or so after the search, Frau Göring informed the company commander that large numbers of valuable items were missing.

That night, shortly after taps, the officers and some senior non-commissioned officers raided the barracks of the soldiers who had searched Veldenstein Castle. Some members of the raiding party were stationed outside the barracks in case some of the loot was thrown out of the windows when the search began. This action proved wise, for many items were hastily tossed out during the search. Other valuables were found stashed in footlockers. It quickly became quickly apparent that Veldenstein Castle had been thoroughly looted.

The most valuable item recovered was Göring's Reichsmarschall Dagger, later described as the Mona Lisa of daggers. Initially, Major Talbot intended to forward the dagger to General George Patton as a souvenir from Göring—compliments of the 90th Division. A day or so after the raid, however, it was later reported that Lieutenant Wallace L. Stephenson went into the commander's office and pleaded for the diamond-encrusted dagger. He told his commanding officer that he wanted to sell the dagger in the United States and buy a chicken farm. The softhearted Talbot, so the story goes, turned over the priceless piece to the lieutenant.

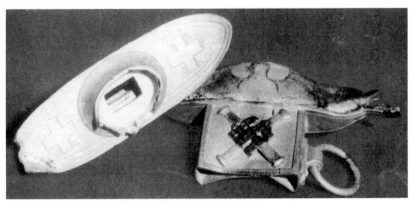

The near-worthless fragments of Göring's Reichsmarschall Dagger after it was demolished by Lieutenant Wallace L. Stephenson. Stephenson's son, Mack, has these items posted on his web site.

Talbot's decision was most unfortunate. Instead of selling the dagger, Stephenson took it home and removed the jewels from it, disassembled what was left, lost the blade, and buried the handle and the few remaining steel parts. Stephenson's son, Mack Stephenson, realized the value of the dagger and in 1992 dug up the few pieces he could find,

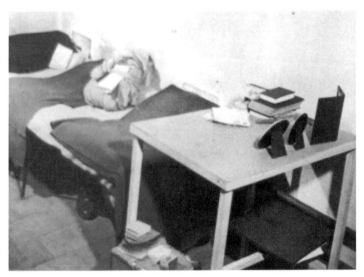

Once one of the most powerful and wealthy men in Europe, by late 1945 Göring's worldly goods fit comfortably in his tiny prison cell. His desk held a photograph of his wife and daughter, a picture of his mother and stepfather, a deck of playing cards, three books, two cigars, and matches.

recovered the jewels, and asked a small fortune for the handful of gems and damaged remains. Portions of this invaluable dagger remain with Mack in Socorro, New Mexico. If this valuable ceremonial weapon was still intact today, it would be worth more than one million dollars.[6]

*   *   *

The International Military Tribunal at Nuremberg tried Göring, along with most of the surviving high ranking German war leaders. The former World War I ace, commander of the Luftwaffe, and art collector was found guilty on all counts and sentenced to death by hanging. Göring, however, had no intention of allowing himself to die in such an undignified manner. Somehow, he managed to obtain a cyanide ampule and poisoned himself on October 15, 1946—just a few hours before his scheduled execution.

In August 1947, Herbert Steward Leonard, of the Monuments Fine Art & Archives in Munich, discovered that Memling's *Madonna With Child* was missing. Leonard wrote the Restitution Branch in Germany that Major Paul Kubala was the last known person in possession of the missing painting, and that Kubala should be questioned as to the location of this rare work of art. At the time, Kubala was in the process of transferring from Germany to the United States. The Criminal Investigation Division (CID) began looking into the matter and discovered that Kubala's household goods had been packed and shipped to Atlantic City, New Jersey. Kubala, meanwhile, notified the New York Port Authorities to ship all of the boxes to him in care of the Transportation Officer at Wright-Patterson Field, Dayton, Ohio.

CID authorities contacted Port officials and asked them to hold the boxes so they could be searched without Kubala's knowledge. The shipment, however, did not arrive together, and one box and one crate had already been sent on to Wright-Patterson. On September 27, 1947, a large trunk and suitcase arrived. A customs inspector and three CID agents broke the steel bands around the two containers and opened them. The agents immediately noticed they had been previously searched or ransacked. A close inspection uncovered silverware, clothing, and female personal effects. The baggage was repacked and resealed. Had Kubala been tipped off about the investigation, and had someone removed the painting and other contraband? On October 20, CID agents inspected the remaining cases. The painting was not found.

Kubala was interrogated about the missing Memling on November 17. The major informed CID agent Lieutenant Colonel William A. Stephens that he could not discuss his assignments due to his role as an Intelligence Agent for the Strategic Services (formerly the Office of Strategic Services, or OSS). When asked about these assignments, Kubala responded: "Sir, I don't know whether I am really free to tell you. I was an agent—top security man—and I don't know whether I am allowed to divulge this information or not." Stephens asked Kubala about the missing *Madonna With Child*. According to Kubala, Göring brought the painting to Seventh Army Headquarters, where it was turned over to a Monuments Fine Art & Archives expert in the presence of Colonel William Quinn. Kubala further stated that he had a receipt in his personal papers from the MFA&A officer for the painting.

Since a receipt would probably clear Kubala, Lieutenant Colonel Stephens allowed him to go to his room and retrieve it. Returning with a number of folders containing his military papers, Kubala searched them for fifteen minutes without success. Kubala told Stephens that he would look through his other personal possessions for the slip of paper. After answering a few more questions, Kubala suggested that Colonel Quinn be interrogated. At the end of the session Stephens told Kubala not to discuss the investigation with anyone.

Irritated with Kubala's response to the interrogation and his "OSS (O So Secret)" attitude, the investigator wrote:

> Kubala is an individual whose character of integrity is sometimes questionable in that he appears to entertain illusions of grandeur and is prone to exaggerate his experiences and accomplishments, particularly those occurring during the hostilities period in the last war.[7]

From September 23-25, the CID agent—without Kubala's knowledge—opened his locked office desk and three-combination lock safe and reviewed all of Kubala's personal and official papers. The papers indicated that he had been "in difficulties" on several occasions. One case resulted in a full-blown investigation of Kubala's activities by Seventh Army CID. This particular investigation resulted in formal charges and the delivery of testimony from both prosecution and defense witnesses.

One of the many charges Kubala was accused of was stealing fifteen gold watches from one of Göring's aides, together with two valuable cigarette cases from Wilhelm Ohnesorge, one of Hitler's old cronies. Kubala also was accused of stealing 87,800 Reichsmarks ($8,780, 1945 value) and wrongfully possessing and converting to his own use property of various military personnel and civilians. Other charges claimed he wrongfully cursed, beat and had sex with female prisoners, and wrongfully cohabited with a woman not his wife openly and in view of the members of his command. (On April 14, 1946, Kubala married the woman, Odile and the following January she gave birth to their child.)

Kubala was obviously in serious trouble, but it helped to have friends in high places. A detailed letter on his behalf from Colonel William Quinn to General Geoffrey Keys, commanding general of the Seventh Army may have saved Kubala from a courts-martial. In that letter of November 3, 1945, Quinn wrote, "Undoubtedly the charges are true; however . . . as you probably guess, I have a warm spot in my heart for Kubala. . . . I would appreciate very much your talking to this man, Geoff, and if you can, try to look at him through my eyes." Keys, in turn, wrote a memorandum authorizing punishment under the 104th Article of War if Kubala agreed to accept that rather than undergo a trial by courts-martial. Kubala endorsed the memorandum on the back, stating that he would accept punishment under the 104th Article of War.[8]

Colonel Quinn, who was by this time serving in the Pentagon, took some of the suspicion off Kubala when he was questioned by CID agents. Kubala, claimed the colonel, was not responsible for the disappearance of *Madonna with Child*. The colonel identified the MFA&A expert who had taken Memling's painting from the office in May 1945 as 40-year-old Lt. James J. Rorimer. Valuables worth millions were taken from high-ranking Nazi officers across Europe, explained Quinn, but the Memling was the only painting confiscated by Seventh Army headquarters.

Quinn's information focused the investigation for the lost painting on Rorimer, who was now Curator of the Cloisters, Metropolitan Museum in New York City. (He was later elected Director of the Metropolitan Museum of Art.) On January 25, 1948, Rorimer gave agents of the 10th CID, New York, a five-page written statement. He had taken possession of the painting from Colonel Quinn on May 17, 1945, he explained, and on May 19, traveled to Berchtesgaden and turned over the Memling to Major John (Jack) H. Smith of the 101st Airborne Division. Rorimer had a receipt from Captain Harry Anderson for the delivery of *Madonna with Child*. Rorimer also produced a photograph showing both Smith and Anderson holding the painting in the sunlight in order to admire its details. This statement seemed to absolve both Kubala and Quinn of having had anything to do with the missing painting; Rorimer, Quinn, and Kubala, after all, were essentially telling the same story.

The CID agents went looking for John (Jack) H. Smith. They started in Detroit, where he was employed by the *Detroit Times* prior to entering military service in 1942. After his stint ended in June 1947, Smith had returned to the *Detroit Times* for a couple of months and then moved to Washington, D.C., where he took a job with *International News Photos*. He was interviewed there by the CID Military District of Washington. Following this interrogation on March 5, 1948, Chief Warrant Officer Jason Benjamin wrote a report, which contained the following:

> An interview with John Jack H. Smith revealed that some time during May 1945, he received from Colonel William Quinn a painting that was to be photographed. Smith described the painting to the best of his knowledge as being approximately ten by sixteen inches. After photographing the painting, he returned it to Colonel Quinn. Smith added that the negative of the painting photo was sent to the Army Signal Corps Library in Washington.[9]

A meticulous search failed to uncover a Seventh Army photograph of the Memling. Smith's statement contradicted those given by Kubala, Quinn, and Rorimer.

By this time, both Smith and Harry Anderson had been discharged from the army, and as civilians, were no longer under the jurisdiction of the military. When the results of this investigation were sent to the CID office in the European Command, the originator of the investigation, Herbert S. Leonard, had other pressing problems to deal with. His new investigations concerned lost artwork stolen from Italy, as well as the status of priceless pieces removed from Austria. Leonard simply did not have the time or the resources to search for a single piece of art, even if it was a Memling. On March 24, 1948, the case was closed.

Memling's small 6 x 10 inch *Madonna With Child* was never recovered.

- Chapter Five -

The Looting of Berchtesgaden

he scenic Alpine village of Berchtesgaden, located in the Obersalzberg mountains, is where Hitler bought a home in 1933. He renamed it the Berghof. As time passed, the Obersalzberg area grew into a complex of Nazi homes for party higher-ups, complete with security buildings for SS guards. In the end, Berchtesgaden turned out to be one of the most lucrative areas in Germany for pillaging by American troops in the closing days of World War II.

When the Americans arrived at Berchtesgaden, some of the ruins and heavy green camouflage nets draping over most of the buildings were still smoking from fires ignited by British bombing attacks. Hundreds of tall slender pines, which thickly covered the estate, lay broken like match sticks from the concussion of the bombs. Sections of the woods were stripped bare from direct hits. Tiny waterfalls from the hills rippled over the debris field of paper, books, bricks, stone, and other bits of trash and rubble. "It looks to me" said an infantry colonel, "like they were expecting to defend this place with wine bottles."[1]

The steep and winding road leading up to what had been Hitler's mountain retreat above Berchtesgaden was jammed with traffic. American soldiers and French troops on foot and in jeeps, trucks, and swanky captured limousines were going to and from the Berghof and the

The Berghof, Hitler's mountain retreat, before (left), and after (below) British Lancaster bombers plastered the area.

vast expanse of buildings and grounds surrounding it. The Americans and French were staging a celebration on the rubble-littered grounds and buildings that Hitler had built. There was much to celebrate, and a lot to celebrate with, for the wine cellars of the Berghof—especially the cellar of the guest house—contained thousands of bottles of fine French and German wines, cognac, and champagne. In the storerooms of the guest house were

Hitler and Göring in Obersalzberg prior to World War II hostilities.
The leather vest sported by Göring was taken by a soldier at the end
of the war, and is today in the West Point Military Museum.

enough dishes, silverware, and frozen and canned foods to last for years.
One of the servants said the food could last for ten years, "or until the war
had been decided." Unfortunately for the Germans, the war had already
been decided, and the wine, food, silverware, and countless other items
were disappearing with amazing speed.

American soldiers entering the Bavarian village of Berchtesgaden.

Soldiers of the 3rd Division celebrate at a tea room in Hitler's
Eagle's Nest atop Kehlstein Mountain at Berchtesgaden.

The scene at Berchtesgaden was one of bedlam. Moroccans in red
fezzes carried away enormous portraits, which they were almost certain
to toss away in a short time. Americans on foot carried bottles that they
were almost certain to drink within a few hours or days. In fact, there
were many who had already accepted the late Führer's hospitality and
had drunk heavily. The grounds of this once-lovely estate were strewn
with empty bottles that had once held exquisite Burgundies, Moselles,
champagnes, and other vintage wines.

A French truck rumbled down the road. From a chain on its rear hung
a doe recently caught in the woods. Blood was still dripping from its
throat. The French driver and passengers grinned, shouted, and waved
bottles of wine in the air in celebration of the war's end. A sleek, black
Mercedes, Hitler's powerful six-wheel touring car, was jammed into the

Hermann Göring's Obersalzberg home (above), in more peaceful times, and after the British bombing run (below) in 1945.

ditch beside the road. The automobile had been caught suddenly by an air attack, but was being moved out of the way because it was impeding the flow of traffic.

A Bechstein grand piano sat amid the ruins of the great banquet hall, where the *Gauleiters* of the Nazi party had once formulated their political programs. An American sat at its keys, the incongruous sounds of "Deep in the Heart of Texas" filling the once-grand hall. Thousands of glass fragments—all that remained of a huge picture window that had once offered onlookers an unsurpassed view of the Obersalzberg mountains—littered the floor. The scene was now one of chaos and confusion. And many seized on the opportunity to pilfer what was left of value.

On May 5, 1945, Lieutenant Warren H. Eckberg and Lieutenant Colonel Willard White, members of the 1269th Combat Engineers of the U.S. Seventh Army, acquired many valuable items during their extensive treasure hunt in Berchtesgaden. Eckberg helped himself to a few of Hermann Göring's belongings, including a silver baton covered with 20 miniature imperial German eagles, and 20 Iron Crosses. The top of the baton contained a wreath and German eagle made from diamond chips. The base was silver with black enamel bearing the Iron Cross. The baton was inscribed: "[From] The Führer to the First Field Marshal General of the Air Force." Another item picked up by Eckberg was a solid gold medallion hanging from a large ½-inch thick gold chain. The face of the oval medallion was a crystal enameled coat of arms rimmed with 60 small diamonds. The obverse side contained a gold swastika with 17 diamonds.

Reichsmarschall Hermann Göring's treasured baton, grabbed by Lieutenant Eckberg, is today in the National Infantry Museum, Fort Benning, Georgia.

The Carold-Wilhelminia Institute, an engineering college, presented this gold medallion set, with diamonds, to Hermann Göring (left). Lieutenant Warren H. Eckberg took the medallion from Berchtesgaden in May 1945. The classified ad (below) was placed in the Chicago newspaper for the sale of the Carold-Wilhelminia Institute gold medallion, presented to Hermann Göring.

There exists some confusion regarding Eckberg's looted baton, and Göring's prized baton that had been appropriated by General Patch. Many have assumed that Göring only had one baton, since it was the symbol of the rank and command of a German field marshal. The baton taken by Patch, however, was white, while Eckberg's baton was black. Except for this obvious difference, the batons are identical. The black baton was awarded to Göring as the First Field Marshal General of the Air Force on February 4, 1938; the white baton was awarded on July 19, 1940, in celebration of his promotion to Reichsmarschall of Greater Germany.

Eckberg mailed the medallion, baton, and iron crosses to his mother in Chicago. He remained in the army in Europe and his mother later sold the medallion to a Chicago jeweler. The jeweler placed a classified ad in the Chicago newspaper for the sale of the medallion. U.S. Customs, however, read the ad and as a result, the medallion and baton were confiscated and turned over to the U.S. Army.[2]

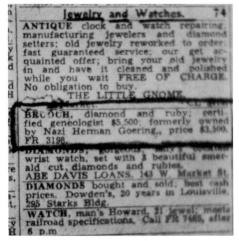

Lieutenant Colonel Willard White, Eckberg's commander, was a strong

These valuable pieces of art and other treasures were removed by American soldiers from "Aladdin's Cave" and placed outside Hermann Göring's underground bunker. The baton in the hands of Sergeant Robert Thibodaux (above) was presented to Göring by Italian Field Marshall Italo Balbo. Lieutenant Colonel Willard White, President Lyndon B. Johnson's brother-in-law, realized the unique value of the baton and later sold the item to noted collector Ben Curtis (opposite page), who is seen holding it.

candidate for top souvenir collector at Berchtesgaden. White took a fortune in spoils that included more than 100 pieces of Hitler's silverware. This silverware—along with silver teapots, silver coffee pots, silver creamers, sugar and gravy dishes, salt and pepper shakers, large silver trays, and covered dishes—were all distinguished by the German

eagle surmounting a swastika and the initials "A H." White

This 14K gold Pilots Badge with Diamonds, made for Hermann Göring, contains 170 diamonds. It was purchased from an American soldier who brought it home at the end of the war. The last known asking price was $75,000.

also obtained some of Hitler's personal stationary, fine quality wool blankets, Dresden figurines, delicate porcelain, and a large collection of German officer swords. He also acquired china and crystal goblets that Göring had stolen from the palace of Louis Napoleon. White sent these valuables to his wife, the sister of Congressman (and future president) Lyndon B. Johnson. After the war, the Whites maintained a grand style of living by gradually selling off this extensive collection.[3] From White's widow, collector Ben Curtis of Dallas, Texas, purchased a jeweled hunting dagger that had belonged to Göring. The dagger is today worth over $75,000.

From "Aladdin's Cave," Thibodaux also walked off with Göring's wedding sword that was presented to him on his second marriage to Emmy Sonneman in April 1935. This unique sword is today owned by Stuart Wilson, a British citizen, and is valued at $500,000.

The original wedding sword was too heavy for Göring so he had a duplicate sword constructed from the finest material available. The blade was from a sword crafted for Napoleon. In 1945, the sword was taken by Major Gene L. Brown, 101st Airborne, from Fischhorn Castle at Zell am See, Austria. As an S-2 Intelligence Officer, Brown searched through several trunks containing Göring's personal belongings. He located the sword and, claiming it was of no particular military significance, kept it. Frau Göring told another story. According to the Reichsmarschall's wife, an American officer appeared at Fischhorn Castle and told her that her husband was being released the following day, and would be returning to

the castle. In her elation, she gave the officer the valuable duplicate sword. When she realized she had been duped, Frau Göring complained to the authorities to no avail. Today, the

Charles Lindbergh, America's most famous aviator, is seen here with Göring admiring his Wedding Sword in the summer of 1936.

A close-up shot of the Obverse of Göring Wedding Sword.

sword is owned by noted collector Stephen Wolfe. It is valued at $600,000.

White and Eckberg were not the only ones who came away from the Obersalzberg retreat with quality items. John C. Porter, from Troy, Michigan, was exploring Berchtesgaden when he discovered that Hermann Göring's home had taken a direct bomb hit that had blown part of the house into the patio and reflecting pool. The pool was full of debris, including two human bodies, and was covered with a thin layer of ice. As Porter looked into the water, the sun reflected off something lying on the bottom of the pool. Although the water was freezing cold, Porter removed his clothes and dove into the pool. By the time he surfaced he was the proud owner of a French ceremonial Roman Gladius-style sword, crafted by

This lovely sword (right) was presented to Göring by Italy's fascist leader Benito Mussolini, and was found and removed from "Aladdin's Cave." Today, this invaluable specimen is in the National Infantry Museum, Fort Benning, Georgia.

A close-up view the sword presented to Göring by Mussolini.

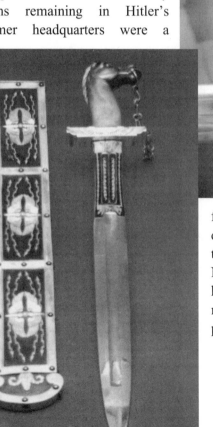

Boutet, Napoleon Bonaparte's personal armoire. Porter took the sword with him and later sold it to a private collector in 1978 for an undisclosed sum.[4]

Several days after the capture of Berchtesgaden, Colonel Bernard Bernstein visited the Berghof and noticed that the only items remaining in Hitler's former headquarters were a fireplace and toilet. "How can I dismantle the fireplace, remove the toilet, and ship them back to New York?" he thought to himself. "They would both make a great conversation piece." Bernstein did not act on

The Roman Gladius-style sword found in Göring's pool (left) was probably originally pilfered from a French museum by the Reichsmarschall.

While Colonel Bernstein did not dismantle Hitler's fireplace, this ceramic tile was one of hundreds removed from the fireplace by an overzealous souvenir hunter of the 101st Airborne. The tiles on Hitler's fireplace at the Berghof depicted different scenes of the Third Reich and Hitler's rise to power.

his thoughts, the colonel was one of the few individuals who left Obersalzberg empty-handed.[5]

One of the more fascinating items found at the Obersalzberg was a gold watch belonging to Dr. Theodor Morell, Hitler's personal and most trusted physician. While guarding a valuable electronic microscope in Morell's laboratory, H. R. Ira, 101st Airborne, searched through Morell's belongings and found the watch that had been given to the doctor on his birthday by the Führer. The timepiece chimes every 15 minutes, and is engraved: "On July 22, 1944 with my Heartfelt Wishes," with a facsimile signature of Adolf Hitler. Ira brought the watch home and the Army shipped the Siemens microscope and other valuable scientific equipment to RCA Victor, Camden N. J. The solid gold pocket watch is today in the private collection of the prestigious collector Thomas T. Wittmann.

Another pocket watch found here, this one crafted of white gold, was presented to SA Chief of Staff Victor Lutze by Italian General L. Russo. This exceptional watch was made by the prestigious Italian firm Bvlgari, and is adorned around the circumference with blue sapphire gemstones. The reverse side is engraved with the Latin spelling of Lutze's first name, "Vittorio." After the murder of Ernst Roehm in the Blood Purge of 1934, Lutze was appointed Roehm's successor and remained head of the powerful SA until his death in an automobile accident in 1943. The watch is today in the distinguished collection of Thomas Johnson.

In addition to the Berghof, other home at the Obersalzberg were thoroughly looted by the exhilarated Allies. Members of the 42nd Infantry Division, and a few weeks later members of the American Red Cross Club Mobile, looted Heinrich Himmler's home, Haus Schmeewinkel, built for his 32-year-old mistress Hedwig Potthast and

Dr. Theodor Morell's gold watch, a personal gift from Adolf Hitler.

their two children. Lieutenant
Roland E. Gebbert, Third Army,
removed a bedroom suite complete
with furnishings and a chandelier. He
transported the bedroom to his
officer's quarters and had the
chandelier installed in a conference
room at Third Army Headquarters.
Captain John R. Mitchell removed a
desk and rug and took them also to
Third Army Headquarters. John
Johnson, an American civilian,
acquired a large wooden plaque with
an attached bronze pheasants and
gun. A member of the 506th
Regiment of the 101st pilfered a

The white gold time piece presented to
SA Chief of Staff Victor Lutze by Italian
General L. Russo.

German Social Welfare Decoration Special Class, 1st Class, Ladies' Decoration with Diamonds. Estimated Value $75,000. Found at Klessheim Castle, near Salzburg, Austria. This award was seized from Private Marshal Herrera by U.S. Customs agents.

magnificent 7 x 9 foot one-of-a-kind tapestry that had once hung in the Reichstag.

By the time the Allies had finished, Himmler's home had been completely stripped of its valuable belongings. The most noteworthy works of art of Heinrich Hoffmann, Hitler's photographer, were stolen as was Martin Bormann's art collection, which consisted of more than 1,000 Rudolf Alt watercolors.

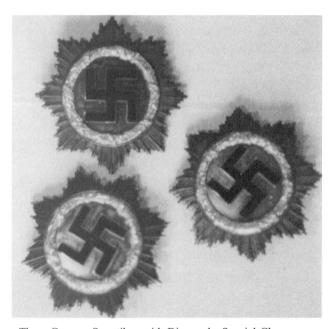

These German Swastikas with Diamonds, Special Class, were never awarded. Estimated value: $25,000 each. These were seized from Private Marshal Herrera by U.S. Customs agents.

*   *   *

Understandably, more valuables were looted during the advance of American troops. Klessheim Castle, near Salzburg, Austria, provided another rich cache for zealous souvenir hunters. The castle had once belonged to the Hapsburg family, but was little more than a standing ruin at the beginning of the Nazi regime. It was completely renovated, furnished, and decorated by the Germans during World War II. Once completed, Klessheim was a jewel, and used to entertain visiting celebrities. It was there that Hitler met Benito Mussolini to discuss Fascist strategy shortly after the surrender of Italy to the Allies in 1943. After the capture of Klessheim by the 3rd Infantry Division, Marshal P. Herrera was assigned the task of removing camouflage, mines, and booby traps from the castle. During the assignment, he found a large collection of valuable objects stored in the basement. Herrera acquired proper certification, found a wooden box, and mailed the items home. Later, U.S. Customs seized the more valuable medals.

Herrera, however, was allowed to keep a Nazi flag, knife, fork, and spoon.

Chapter Six

Sepp Dietrich's Souvenirs

Rolf Wartenberg, former German citizen turned U.S. Army captain, was in charge of the Reception Camp at the Seventh Army Interrogation Center. The captain managed to acquire a valuable one-of-a-kind saber that belonged to notorious SS General Josef "Sepp" Dietrich.

Dietrich, who rose to fame as the commander of Hitler's SS bodyguard, and later as the leader of an elite SS Panzer Army, was born in 1892. After service in World War I, Dietrich gained experience in the *Freikorps*, suffered through a prolonged period of unemployment, and engaged in a string of petty crimes associated with the SA. By 1928, he was a full-fledged member of the notorious SS. Although he carved out an enviable battlefield record in the invasion of France, fighting in the Balkans, and on the Eastern Front, charges of criminal conduct—such as the slaughter of Russian prisoners and wounded at Kharkov—followed him through much of his career. Dietrich, a hot-tempered soldier with a foul mouth, spearheaded the failed armoured offensive in the Battle of the Bulge. His last assignment was in Hungary defending Vienna, where Russian forces overwhelmed his command. Knowing what the Russians would do to him if he was captured by them, Dietrich moved west in May of 1945 with the hope of surrendering to the Americans.

Sepp Dietrich, commander of the Sixth SS Panzer Army, during a frivolous moment with Hilde, the daughter of Albert Speer.

The SS officer and his wife were arrested by the U.S. Military and brought to the U.S. Seventh Army Headquarters, where they were assigned to Rolf Wartenberg for interrogation. The accommodating Wartenberg arranged for Frau Dietrich to remain with her husband, who was soon transferred to another camp.

On his day off, Wartenberg drove Frau Dietrich to her hometown. As a "gift," she offered Wartenberg her husband's shotgun collection. When they arrived at Dietrich's home, however, she discovered that vandals had looted the collection. Wartenberg asked if she had any more weapons in the house. She hesitated for a few moments, went down into the basement, and returned with her husband's SS honor sword. As the respected commander of the *Liebstandarte SS Adolf Hitler* (Hitler's bodyguard), Dietrich had been presented this rare sword with a Damascus blade. His wife opened the case and removed the sword. With a tear in her eye, she kissed the blade, returned it to the case, and presented it to Wartenberg.[1]

The sword remained in Wartenberg's possession until September 1983, when he sold it to a private Texas collector. Today, the sword—valued at more than $250,000—is in the prestigious collection of Thomas Johnson.

Sepp Dietrich was tried eventually for war crimes by a United States court and sentenced to life in prison. He served less than a decade behind

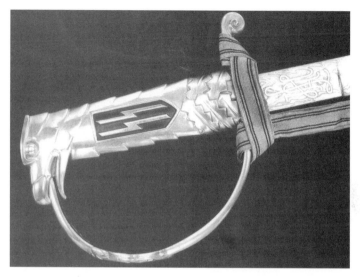

Sepp Dietrich's Damascus sword, presented by his men for his role as the respected commander of the *Liebstandarte SS Adolf Hitler*.

bars before being secretly released in October 1955. He died of a heart attack in 1966 as a free man—a far better fate than he deserved.

Sepp Dietrich was not the only high-ranking Nazi Rolf Wartenberg came into contact with at Seventh Army Interrogation Center. During his stay there, Hermann Göring offered Wartenberg his accordion as a souvenir. Wartenberg, who still has the instrument, recalls that Göring was too fat to hold and play it.

Sepp Dietrich's document award for his Knights Cross of the Iron Cross. The cases for this and related awards are in the West Point Military Academy Museum. The awards were issued on December 31, 1941, and March 14, 1943, and signed by Adolf Hitler.

At the end of the World War II, Lieutenant Warren W. Knauss and his 80th Infantry Division was in Braunau, Austria. While investigating a citizen's compliant of robbery, he discovered that the house was loaded with trunks. The cases were opened, and in one of them Knauss found Sepp Dietrich's Russian winter coat, boots, cap, and documentation for his Knight Cross and associated decorations. The cases holding the citations are blue pigskin with topazes set in gold. Knauss sent the items home, and in 1967 presented them to the West Point Museum. (Coincidentally, Braunau, Austria, was the birthplace of Adolf Hitler. It escaped serious damage during the war.)

Dietrich's winter coat worn during the fighting on the Eastern Front, found in a truck in a house in Braunau, Austria.

Chapter Seven

The Military Governor of Weimar

During the war, the U.S. Army trained and placed older American men into civil affairs organizations and military government positions in order to prepare for the occupation of Axis countries. The men were typically between 38 and 46 years old, and were usually lawyers, public safety officials, or financial experts.

Lieutenant Colonel William M. Brown entered military service on October 8, 1917, and served in the United States in several reserve positions until he returned to active duty on August 15, 1942. He taught military government at Fort Custer and the University of Wisconsin, where he was also an instructor in languages. Brown was fluent in several tongues, including French and German. After transferring overseas on January 1, 1944, he became a member of the instructional staff at Shrivenham, England. Brown spent most of this period at Trirlemont, Belgium, where he trained more military government detachments than any other officer in the entire European theater of operations. He was awarded the Bronze Star for his work.

On April 1, 1945, Brown transferred into Germany and reported to Lieutenant Colonel Strom Thurmond, who later served as governor of South Carolina and currently sits as a U.S. senator. In 1945, Thurmond was operations officer of G-5, First Army. He asked Brown to assist him in drafting detachment rosters and assigning personnel to posts that

Lieutenant Colonel Brown was a 51-year-old military officer. As we shall see, the former Republican candidate for governor of Virginia tacitly accepted the theory that "loot, lust, and liquor" were the rewards of the victorious soldier.

needed immediate attention. On April 24, Brown's Military Government Unit 71 was assigned the city and county of Weimar, the concentration camp at Buchenwald, and the city of Apolda. To assist Colonel Brown, the Army hired Kurt J. Vogler, a German who had lived in the United States from 1921 to 1939.

The investigation at Buchenwald was massive. The American press was engaged in the odious task of photographing and filming the horrors of the concentration camp. Hundreds of people, including senators, congressmen, army officers, and civilians from virtually every Allied country traveled to Buchenwald. Displaced persons arrived and made demands for food and housing. Brown gave Vogler the assignment of finding cameras to give to the press as complimentary gifts from the military government. From the camera shop of A. Spieler in Weimar, Vogler took three Leicas, one Contax and one Rolliflex. Vogler signed a receipt for the cameras and told Spieler that the U.S. military government wanted to use the cameras for about three weeks and would return them to his shop. The loan of the cameras would make it possible for his shop to open sooner so he could resume business, or so Vogler informed him.

On April 24, a notice was issued to the population of Weimar that all cameras were to be surrendered to the military government. About fifteen additional cameras were obtained through this directive. They were turned over to Brown and he gave the requested cameras to the United Press as gifts. As Brown later admitted, "The cameras were under the first proclamation I issued—all subject to confiscation, just like firearms. I believe every officer and enlisted man was asking for cameras and other souvenirs that they might take home. There was no reimbursement to the owners of the cameras, because there was not supposed to be any."

On May 5, Brown, Lieutenant William M. Crowe, and Vogler made an inspection of the city and surrounding areas. Brown noticed that the Weimar post office had been badly damaged by bombs. The main entrance was boarded up and off-limits signs were posted at the entrances. The U.S. Signal Corps had taken over a portion of the building for living quarters and had converted the post office's telephone exchange, using it for the U.S. Army signal exchange. Brown and his party entered the building and found a number of German postal employees inside. Spotting some stamps, Brown took a large number as he left the post office. He also gave orders prohibiting all postal officials from entering the building.

Thereafter, Brown suspended the activities of the German post office in Weimar and confiscated its funds and assets. Lieutenant Crowe, the labor, finance, and property control officer, Private Joseph A. Dougherty, and PFC Willis J. Herman, went to the post office, picked up all the packages and mail, and transported them to the military government detachment. A return trip was made to pick up the currency. They loaded all the Reichsmarks and stamps onto a truck. The money and stamps were not counted, and there were no receipts given to the German postal officials—even when they requested one. The postal authorities' balance books later showed that 195,000 Reichsmarks (or $19,500, 1945 value) had been seized from the post office. The valuables were taken to the headquarters of the military government detachment and placed on a table upstairs in Colonel Brown's office. Brown entered a few moments later, opened a safe, and put the money inside without counting it. Just prior to Brown's entering the office, Private Dougherty took a cellophane-wrapped package of German currency containing 50 twenty-mark notes. Private Herman helped himself to a pair of the twenty-mark packages. Three thousand marks had been removed from the postal funds.

A few days later the chief of the Weimar post office wrote Brown a letter requesting that the currency be returned. He explained that the money represented purchased money orders and questioned whether the confiscation was justified under the U.S. Occupation law. As might be expected, there was no response to his request.

On May 10, Brown and Vogler went to see Hans Müller and his brother, Wilhelm Müller. During the war Hans, a passionate Nazi, strode about town with a walking stick and greeted everyone with a crisp Nazi salute. Because of his friendship with Karl Koch, Buchenwald's commander, and other high-ranking members of the Nazi party, Müller was able to become the proud owner of the largest and most expensive jewelry store in Weimar.

Brown purchased seven diamond rings and paid for them with German Reichsmarks. These rings cost about $2,200. He also purchased a four-and-half carat diamond ring for $1,200, and then went upstairs and purchased cut glass, a silver bread basket, and six silver tea cups with silver saucers. During the month, Brown hauled off several more purchases from Müller's shop, promising to make payment at a later date.

A pre-war photo of Schiller Street, Weimar. Hans Müller's jewelry store is near the car on the right side of the street.

Müller recorded Brown's "purchases." The colonel told Hans Müller that he could not pay for the items right away, and that he would have to transfer the money to Europe from a bank in New York using the American Express Company. During this credit transaction Müller, sensing that he would not be paid, only commented that "I will be glad that I sell it now. When the Russians come in I will lose it anyway."[1]

The valuables were carefully packed in six large wooden boxes so that Brown could mail them back to the States. All of the costly items would disappear before the Americans left Weimar.

Although Brown made the purchases personally, the articles were billed to the military government's officers' club. To pay the bills, Brown opened his safe and took out the German marks. He turned the confiscated currency over to Vogler and instructed him to pay, which he did, except for a small sum to satisfy a debt of $60.50 to Müller. Brown also gave Vogler authority to purchase liquor from Gustav Giesel, a wine wholesaler. Purchases were to be billed to the account of the military government. From April 29 until June 26, 1945, Giesel delivered 8,723 bottles of German and French wine and one barrel of corn liquor to the military government's headquarters building. The shipment was then taken to the private residence of Lieutenant Colonel Brown. During the purchase Vogler took 113 bottles of wine and seven bottles of liquor for his own use.

In a request for payment, Giesel wrote the following rather garbled plea to the police in Weimar:

> In spite of having delivered all my wines to the Americans through Vogler, my location was seized with the whole furniture removed. I got permission to stay in the attic. But since June 5, I was forced to move from my attic and must live in a small shed located on my grounds. My wife is older than 60 and I myself older than 70 years. In this little shed lives my unmarried ill son. By this time my wife is unable to take care of my son, but which is absolutely necessary.
>
> The only idea I have belonging to the removal of my family of the attic of my house is, that this was done by Mr. Vogler whom to separate me from them and who wanted to give me a depression. I hope the American military government will be able to understand my request to stay in the attic of my house and will soon give the permission as to this question.[2]

Giesel had signed bills, statements and other business documents to prove that he had sold the U.S. military government 12,432 Reichsmarks ($1,243) worth of liquor on credit. He never received a penny of payment.

In the course of business Brown mentioned to Vogler that he collected stamps, and asked him to find out if any local prominent Nazi officials were stamp collectors. Vogler's investigation on this subject revealed that a man named Henschel at Preller Street 9 had a large collection and had been recently arrested by the American CIC. Vogler went to see Frau Henschel, who told him that the stamps were in a safe deposit box in the Deutsche Bank. Vogler later met Frau Henschel at the bank and she withdrew the collection. He took three large packets of stamps from her and gave them to Brown, with Frau Henschel taking the remainder of them home.

Brown, however, continued to hound Vogler for the rest of the collection. "Vogler," Brown told him, "I've got a box here, which private Wahl is packing for me, to be sent home. I hope to get those stamps today."[3] Vogler, taking this as an order, went to Henschel's home once more and told Frau Henschel that the military governor demanded the rest of the stamps, which she quietly turned over to him.

Brown was such an avid stamp collector that he had his secretary remove every stamp from the letters and packages he had seized at the post office. This task took days to accomplish. These stamps, along with the Henschel collection, went in a U.S. mailbag. Brown had informed Vogler he would arrange payment for these items, but compensation was never made.

On May 18, 1945, Brown told Vogler to arrange for the cashing of a bond issued by the Reichsbank of Germany in the sum of 15,000 Reichsmarks. The 3.5 percent Treasury bond had been issued in 1941 with a maturity date of May 16, 1945. Brown had found the allegedly "abandoned" bond and considered it his personal property. Vogler entered the bank after it had closed and introduced himself as the person empowered by the military government to handle all financial transactions in Weimar. The bank explained that they could not cash the bond without the approval of the stock exchange in Berlin. The transaction was also subject to the approval of the U.S. military government.

Vogler, almost as if on cue, began shouting that he had the authority to approve the transaction and demanded that the bond be redeemed immediately. A soldier who had accompanied Vogler verbally affirmed his authority. The bank officials accepted the bond after Vogler signed it and issued him 15,150 Reichsmarks. Vogler turned the money over to Lieutenant Colonel Brown.

On June 6, 1945, Brown's Military Government Detachment 71 was dissolved and relieved by a new detachment, G1C9, in preparation for the Russian occupation. Brown wrote a letter of recommendation for Kurt Vogler. In part it stated that Vogler had been given many assignments of a confidential nature and had performed them all in a satisfactory manner and was recommended for similar employment. Vogler continued to work for the new detachment, although he was used only as an oral translator and not for "investigative" work.

After working with Vogler for several days, Private George H. Hamilton became suspicious of him, largely because German civilians regarded Vogler as a person of considerable authority. Officially, however, Vogler was only an interpreter. After several discrete inquiries were made of civilians, Hamilton concluded that Vogler had assumed considerable authority—and had perhaps even falsified his employment records. The private believed an investigation was needed, and as a result a warrant was issued on June 12, 1945, for Vogler's arrest. Hamilton went to Lieutenant Colonel Brown's residence and informed him that a warrant had been issued for Vogler's arrest. Brown, obviously startled by this development, professed that he had no knowledge of the whereabouts of his German friend.

In fact, Brown was at that very moment waiting for Vogler to arrive with a Frau Wielthaus, a singer who performed regularly in the Weimar Halle Hotel. Brown had directed Vogler to bring her to his home. Shortly after Hamilton departed, about 11:00 p.m., Vogler drove up the driveway accompanied by Wielthaus. Brown immediately escorted Vogler upstairs, advised him of the warrant, and told him to leave town at once. Vogler protested, claiming that he had done nothing that he wished to conceal, that he had a wife and child in Weimar, and that he had no money except for 42 marks. Brown provided Vogler with 1,000 Reichsmarks and told him he would send word to his family so they would not worry about him. The singer, Frau Wielthaus, remained at Brown's house and left the following morning at 5:00 a.m. in his car with his civilian chauffeur, Walter Bernhardt. They picked up her children and drove to Dortmund, her hometown in the occupation zone of East Germany. Fortunately, Wielthaus was able to get her family out of the Russian-controlled area.

Vogler also departed Weimar and spent the night in his car on the outskirts of town. The next morning, however, he returned and reported to the local CIC detachment and was jailed. During the ensuing investigation of his activities, Vogler made a number of incriminating statements about Brown. These incriminating statements led to an investigation of Brown by the Inspector General.

On June 27, 1945, Brown was questioned about his activities while serving as military governor of Weimar. These questions were asked and recorded by Captain Arthur V. Patterson. During questioning, Brown was informed that all property found or confiscated in enemy country belonged to the United States government. His response to this statement was the following:

Well, I am sure that I didn't know that because the general impression at that time was that whatever people picked up—that was immediately after the combat phase—whatever people picked up they were entitled to. You know as well as I do that there's been a good deal of that going on, and there has been a good deal of picking up stuff, abandoned by all troops. Anything of that kind that I was engaged in there was done with the idea that whatever things of that sort were found where there was no claimant whatever, belonged to the finder. To what extent may I ask off the record—well, weren't they, if they were found without any claimant? If you find the stuff lying abandoned, doesn't that belong to you?[4]

Conditions in Weimar immediately following the cessation of hostilities were indeed chaotic. News of the American withdrawal and the Russian occupation made the civilian population hysterical with fear of Russian reprisals in the eastern portion of the country. Because of this impending occupation, Brown was relieved as military governor of Weimar. He had been in command only six weeks. All U.S. personnel and equipment had to be completely removed from Weimar by June 30, because the Russian occupation of Thuringia and Saxony would be effective on July 1, 1945.

Not far from Weimar, the small village of Schwarzburg was occupied by Company F, 406th Infantry Regiment, 102nd Infantry Division. On a hill overlooking the town was Schwarzburg Castle. Its basement was brimming with porcelain and 121 art treasures stored there by the Thuringia State Museum, located in Weimar. Hundreds of paintings from other collections were also stored in the castle, including Tischbein's *Lady Elizabeth*. The stronghold, with its broken windows and shattered doors, was riddled with a number of entrances, but members of Company F guarded only the main entrance.

On June 12, 1945, Dr. Walther Scheidig, Director of the Thuringia State Museum, visited the castle and discovered that the basement depository had been broken into and valuable paintings plundered. It was clear by the footprints of rubber soles with American inscriptions and from the numerous cigarette butts lying about that the intruders had been American soldiers. Scheidig later explained that he reported the loss of two Dürer paintings, *Venus with Amour* by Lucas Cranach, and 11 other valuable pieces of artwork to the Company Commander, Captain Paul N. Estes.

Captain Estes and Lieutenant Colonel Issac A. Gatlin, 2nd Battalion Commander, went to the castle together and noticed Cranach's *Venus*

In July 1995, the missing painting, Tischbein's Lady Elizabeth (left) turned up in a Sotheby's auction. The *Venus* (below) by Lucas Cranach, found its way into a Yale art gallery in the early 1970s and was sold to a Swiss collector, where the trail ends. Barbari's Christ (opposite page) and nine other priceless paintings stolen by an American soldier from the Schwarzburg Castle have never been recovered.

with Amour was missing. The painting was of a youthful nude woman and nude boy with a bee on his forehead and chest. Estes, in a cursory investigation of the missing Cranach described it as "a painting of a child with a fly on its nose, which appeared very real and allegedly valued at one million dollars."[5] The 102nd Infantry Division moved into Bavaria as the Russians occupied Thuringia; Estes forgot the incident.

Years later, on October 21, 1953, Dr. Scheidig (who had

originally reported the theft of the Cranach painting) wrote Ardelia Hall, Monuments and Fine Art Officer of the Department of State, requesting her help in the recovery of the valuables stolen from Schwarzburg Castle. According to Scheidig, the castle had been guarded by troops of the 15th American Infantry Division. Apparently the German authorities were confused at the time over the identification of the division at the castle, because there was no 15th Infantry Division. Scheidig, however, included a sketch of the patch worn by the Americans: it was the 102nd  Infantry Division's insignia. He further reported that Churchill J. Brazelton, who had attended Princeton University and was from Waco, Texas, could assist in the recovery of the missing valuables.

On July 21, 1954, the Army initiated an investigation of the 1945 theft by questioning Captain Paul Estes at his home in Miami, Florida. Estes took a lie detector test that was inclusive. Lieutenant Colonel Issac Gatlin had remained in the Army, and was questioned at Fort Gordon, Georgia. Several former officers of the 102nd were interviewed; each of them reiterated to a man that they were only aware of the missing paintings of a "child with a fly on its nose." In 1955, Ardelia Hall wrote Scheidig that the investigation of ten months had failed to provide any clues that would help to find the missing paintings.

Time solved part of the mystery. In 1966, two small paintings by Albrecht Dürer, both stolen in 1945 from Schwarzburg Castle and worth at least $1 million, turned up in the collection of a New York lawyer. The lawyer, Edward I. Elcofon, reported that in 1946, a man about 25 to 30 years old came to his home claiming "he was sent by a friend of mine."[6]

Coins stolen from the Weimar State Museum during Lieutenant Colonel William Brown's corrupt command tenure.

Underneath his arm was a package containing eight paintings he had bought in Europe. Elcofon picked out the two paintings by Dürer, dickered with the young man over the price, and agreed to pay him $500 for the both of them.

The two small Dürer paintings, portraits of Hans and Felicitas Tucher, were once owned by the Grand Duchess of Sachsen-Weimar. The Federal Republic of Germany obtained a lawyer in New York and filed a claim for the Grand Duchess against Elcofon. After 20 years of legal battles—and in the face of Elcofon's steadfast denials of any wrongdoing—he was forced to turn the paintings over to the U.S. Department of State. It appears as though Elcofon really did not know the value of the paintings: he had an inch cut off one of them so it would fit into an inexpensive matching frame, and he had the paintings displayed in his home.

In 1979, the same 102nd Division's officers that were investigated in 1954 were required by the United States District Court in New York to give sworn affidavits regarding their activities while occupying Schwarzburg Castle. They all stuck by their original story regarding the artwork.

Churchill Brazelton had not been subjected to questioning in 1954. In 1979, however, he was requested to give an affidavit about his activities while in Weimar. Brazelton told the investigating authorities that he met Dr. Scheidig in 1945, they had a mutual interest in antiques and objects of art, and that Scheidig helped him obtain a pair of antique pistols. After the war, Brazelton had made his home in New York. The two Dürers were finally returned to the Thuringia State Museum in 1982.

In 1949, fifty coins from the Weimar City Museum were offered for sale by antique dealer Berry-Hill, East 57th Street, New York. Berry-Hill did not own the collection, but was acting as an agent for another dealer, Gruenthals, which had acquired the collection from a "Colonel Smith" after having been shown a statement from the War Department that everything was in order. The colonel had supposedly won the coins from a Russian general during a poker game. The Weimar museum officials told a different story. They reported that the American commander at Weimar had ordered that the valuables be turned over to him. The museum had packed them into sealed boxes and presented them to the American occupying commander. The following day, the museum director noticed that the boxes had been broken open and that the commander was wearing a valuable antique ring from the collection. Shortly thereafter, the Americans left Weimar and the Russians took over the area as their part of the zone of occupation. Most of the coins have never been recovered.[7]

Chapter Eight

Buried Treasure at Buchenwald

During Lieutenant Colonel William Brown's tenure at Weimar, Major Howard M. McBee, the investigating officer of war crimes from the Judge Advocate Section, went to Buchenwald Concentration Camp to investigate the atrocities and brutal treatment of the prisoners once held there.

Buchenwald, one of Hitler's first concentration camps, was located in a patch of timber outside Weimar. The complex was used to provide forced labor for a variety of armament plants in the vicinity. As horrible as it was—the dead averaged about 6,000 each month—Buchenwald was not an extermination camp. When it was liberated in April 1945 by the U.S. 80th Infantry Division, Buchenwald held 20,000 starving prisoners.

When Major McBee arrived at Buchenwald, two German political prisoners who had worked in the disinfecting plant there told him that a large deposit of valuable property was hidden in a cave at the stone quarry in the western part of the camp. McBee, the two Germans, and two prisoners who had worked in the quarry soon found the location, where two air raid shelters had been dug to form a tunnel. The Germans had covered the tunnel mouths by blasting rocks over the entrances.

Twenty men were dispatched to the quarry to dig out the fallen rock. After three hours of hard work, the men managed to carve a small hole into the entrance of one of the tunnels. Major McBee squeezed through

(Above) The main entrance to Buchenwald. A hand-drawn map (below) with arrows pointing to the location of the entrances to valuables in the stone quarry (Steinbruch), 75 meters from the entrance at Buchenwald.

the narrow opening and discovered several suitcases containing a wide variety of items, including U.S. currency, U.S. gold coins, diamonds, precious stones, clocks, razors, tools, tableware, dishes, and gold fillings

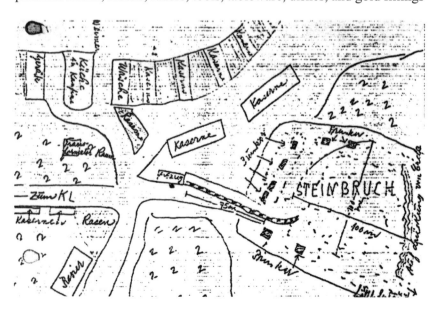

(Below and Left) Some of the thousands of valuables uncovered by the American Army from the notorious Buchenwald Concentration Camp tunnels—including gold fillings removed from murdered victims.

wrenched from the teeth of murdered concentration camp victims. The quarry was immediately placed under the security of the U.S. military while work continued on the mouth of the second tunnel. When the excavation was completed, the retrieved valuables filled nine two-and-one- half ton army trucks. After clearing out the tunnels, the U.S. Army Engineers blasted the entrances closed. A bulldozer finished covering the entrances with rocks so that no one would be injured should the tunnels ever collapse. The loot, which filled 319 boxes, arrived on May 6, 1945, at the Foreign Exchange Depository in Frankfurt.[1]

The American Army turned over to the Inter-Governmental Committee for Refugees (IGCR) millions of dollars' worth of accumulated Nazi SS Loot recovered by the Allies from Buchenwald Concentration Camp, Merkers, and various unsavory individuals. These valuables were eventually shipped to New York City for sale at Gimbel's, Macy's, and other prestigious outlets. When the valuable cargo arrived in

These two lovely necklaces (left and below) were recovered by the American Army from the Buchenwald Concentration Camp, and turned over to the Inter-Governmental Committee for Refugees and subsequently sold in New York.

America, it was quickly discovered that one especially valuable lot of jewelry was missing and presumed stolen. This lot contained the following:

- Forty-Five 14-carat gold chain bracelets in good condition, weighing 1,802 grams;
- Seventeen 14-carat gold bracelets in good condition, weighing 728 grams;
- Two bracelets, one necklace, one purse, one watch chain, all in 18-carat gold, weighing 162 grams;
- Eight fourteen-carat gold extra-long necklaces in good condition, weighing 242 grams;
- Thirty-one 14-carat gold men's watch chains in good condition, weighing 395 grams.

The IGCR advised that it was in communication with its New York representative, who would transmit this information to an insurance company; if further investigation was necessary, the company would advise the Foreign Exchange Depository. Not surprisingly, no one assumed responsibility or blame for the stolen gold, and the investigation was dropped. Nothing was ever recovered.[2]

– Chapter Nine –

Operation Macabre

On April 27, 1945, after the capture of Nordhausen, seven Americans soldiers from the 350th Ordnance Depot inspected the nearby Bernterode Mine for ammunition. The men discovered some 400,000 tons of it in the 15 miles of underground corridors that honeycombed the complex. Their exploration also turned up something else of interest: a masonry wall built into the side of the main corridor a quarter of a mile from the shaft entrance and not far from a large store of dynamite. The mortar holding the wall in place was still fresh.

The men knocked through a portion of the wall and tunneled through masonry and other debris for six feet, when they uncovered a framed latticed door padlocked on the opposite side. Breaking through this, they entered a room with a central passageway and three compartments on either side connecting two large end bays.

Each of these bays were filled with paintings, boxes, and tapestries, all festooned with brilliant banners. The contents were grouped around four caskets, one of which was decorated with a wreath and red silk ribbons bearing the swastika and the name Adolf Hitler.

Captain Walker Hancock was contacted and given the assignment of investigating the discovery. He traveled to Bernterode Mine on April 29, just two days after the secret room was breached. When Hancock crawled

The building in the center is the entrance to the Bernterode Mine, where one of the most amazing discoveries during the final days of WWII was made.

through the opening into the hidden chamber, he was struck with the realization that this was no ordinary depository of works of art. Indeed, the place felt more like a shrine. The objects inside was symmetrically arranged. There was a dramatic display of the splendid colorful banners, all hung in deep rows over the caskets and stacked with a decorative effect in the corners. In each of the three compartments on the right of the central passageway was a wooden coffin, placed parallel to the partition. A label was attached to the top of each coffin with scotch tape. Hastily scrawled in reddish crayon was written "Field Marshall von Hindenburg," "Mrs. von Hindenburg," and "Frederick Wilhelm I, the Soldier King." In the last compartment on the left was a large metal casket with no decorations of any kind. On the simple label stuck to the top were the words "Frederick the Great." Near the casket was a small metal box containing color portraits of military leaders from Frederick Wilhelm I to Hitler. The soldiers who had found the fresh masonry wall in the outer corridor had no way of knowing that they had discovered the resting place of remains of some of Germany's greatest historical figures.

American soldiers loading the heavy casket containing the corpse of Frederick the Great, one of the world's great military leaders.

The 225 banners, which had been so carefully arranged inside, turned out to be Imperial Regimental army standards dating from the early Prussian wars and including many from World War I. Several of the older banners were tattered and mounted upon netting. All were unfurled, contributing to the dramatic display of Prussian militarism.[1]

That evening at army headquarters in Weimar, Captain Hancock made his report and received orders to remove all the contents of the macabre depository. The actual work of packing and hoisting consumed four days and ended on May 8, 1945 (ironically, V-E Day). The caskets were the final items hoisted out of the mine. Frederick the Great's coffin was left for last, since it was anticipated that its great weight and size might cause some trouble. The Americans wanted to make sure that the paintings and other valuable objects were safely out of the mine should the elevator break. Captain Hancock had the unique experience of riding up in the elevator with Field Marshal Paul Ludwig Hans von Hindenburg's remains. Hindenburg, who died in 1934 at Neudeck, his estate in East Prussia, had been one of Germany's finest generals of World War I. He was elected president of Germany in 1925 and again in 1932. It was Hindenburg who had appointed Hitler in 1933 to the position

Hundreds of army standards dating from the early Prussian wars. Twenty-seven of the more valuable standards taken by the American Army are still missing.

of Chancellor on the advice of Franz von Papen, a serious mistake which gave Hitler a position of legitimate power he had long been seeking.

When Hancock reached the surface, the elevator was sent back down into the mine to retrieve Frederick the Great's coffin. The artifact weighed at least twelve hundred pounds; if it had been even one-half inch longer, not even the engineers could have squeezed it aboard. For more than an hour Hancock waited while the men heaved and pulled the casket into the elevator for the ride back to daylight. Meanwhile, a radio installed in the office alongside the shaft entrance poured forth patriotic speeches and music in celebration of the Allied victory in Europe.

When the signal came, the men—all in a jubilant mood—began hoisting as slowly as the engines would turn. It was at this very moment, while Frederick the Great's remains were being lifted to ground level, that the radio began playing the Star Spangled Banner! When the casket of the Prussian king rose to the earth's surface, the tune changed to "God Save the King." Fate could not have designed a better twist of irony for one of history's greatest captains.[2]

Early the next morning a convoy of eight trucks and two jeeps, without escort, started on its journey to the Marburg Collection Point, a place of safekeeping for the macabre cargo. Some have asked why the U.S. Army went to such length to remove the remains from the mine. Why not leave the corpses and let the Russians do the heavy work? One of the answers has its roots in politics. The army knew that the Nordhausen area was about to be turned over to the Russians; lingering distrust and friction between the erstwhile allies was already festering. The political breach that was about to split apart the Western allies and the Russians was already playing itself out. Beating the Russians out of the historical remains of Germany's former leaders was just one example.

In April 1946, the MFA&A received a brief message from General Lucius Clay, the military governor of Germany and the commander of U.S. Forces in Europe. The four distinguished corpses recovered from the Bernterode Mine were going to get a suitable and dignified burial that would reflect honorably on the U.S. government. The assignment was given to the MFA&A personnel because of the historical significance attached to the remains. The project was dubbed, appropriately enough, "Operation Bodysnatch." The entire operation was considered Top Secret.

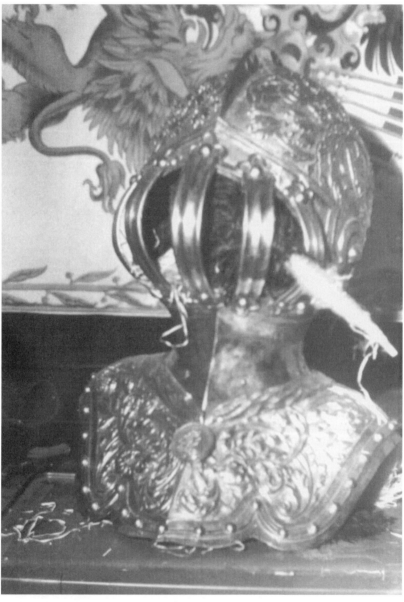

The Helmet (Totenhelm) used in the funeral of the Great Kürfurst in 1688. This beautiful artifact, also found in the Bernterode salt mine by the U.S. Army in April 1945, is valued at over $1,000,000.

The Hindenburg estate was in the British zone of occupation, and a request was made to bury the Field Marshal and his wife there. The British were distressed at the prospect and hastily referred the matter to the Foreign Office in London. With the matter of the Hindenburgs firmly mired in red tape, the MFA&A officers began looking for a site where Frederick Wilhelm I and Frederick Wilhelm II could be buried. The kings were of the Hohenzollern family and two suitable plots of their land were found. The area was in the French occupation zone. When permission was requested from the French, the answer was an unequivocal "no."

The MFA&A officers encountered more obstacles and delays as they continued investigating other Hohenzollern property and various Protestant churches. They finally discovered a church that seemed ideal. It was located just across the street from the Marburg Collection Point, which was where the bodies were concealed. The St. Elizabeth Church had been used for centuries as a burial place for royal families of the region and had somehow managed to escape serious war damage. Two separate sites in the church were selected for the final resting place, and approval was obtained from surviving family members.

In the midst of these burial negotiations, German authorities voiced strenuous objections to the entire plan. Germany's misfortunes, they claimed, were as attributable to Field Marshal von Hindenburg as to Hitler. Although they did not offer the same objection with regard to the two kings, they made it abundantly clear that burial in a church yard was too good for any of the four deceased. In addition the Germans resented having the Hohenzollern and Hindenburg corpses handled by the MFA&A officers. After days of exhausting disagreement, however, the Allies had had enough. The burials, they informed the Germans, would take place as planned.

The coffins were secretly transferred at night and lowered into freshly prepared graves, which were then sealed with a layer of steel and cement. A large sandstone slab was laboriously pushed over the cover of the tombs. The Allies were making it virtually impossible for the disgruntled Germans to remove the coffins. That night a stonecutter chiseled simple inscriptions on the slabs, including names, birth, and death dates—but and no titles. The MFA&A officers congratulated each other on how well the secret had been kept, but by the following morning

The bodies of Field Marshall Paul von Hindenburg and his wife Gertrud are today interned in St. Elisabeth Church. After the unification of Germany, the remains of Frederick Wilhelm I and his nephew were returned to their original burial site in Sans Souci, Potsdam.

more than 500 Germans had gathered at the church. Sixteen months had passed since the bodies had been removed from the Bernterode Mine.[3]

* * *

After the suicide of Hermann Göring and the executions of Hans Frank and other leading Nazi leaders at Nuremberg, it was rumored that their bodies were cremated at Dachau and the ashes strewn into potholes in the main roads around Munich. While no one knows for sure what happened to their remains, we do know that the corpses of the so-called "martyrs" of the Munich Putsch of November 9, 1923, were disinterred and buried elsewhere.

These sixteen bodies had been enshrined in two Temples of Honor (Ehrentempel) at the Königsplatz in Munich. On July 9, 1945, the remains were dug up and interred in family plots in various locations

pursuant to orders that no more than two of the sixteen bodies could be buried in a single location. The 7,532 pounds of tin from the sarcophagi was smelted and used by the city of Munich for maintenance work of

(Above) The Temples of Honor at the Königsplatz in Munich. (Left) The burial vaults of the "martyrs."

streetcars, buses, and other repair work. The iron from the ceremonial pylons was smelted into 453 pig irons weighing some 42,000 pounds, and then promptly "lost." The U.S. Army searched for the missing iron and finally concluded "that no part of the metal in question fell into the hands of a Nazi or fanatic German." The Ehrentemple, which was built with solid concrete and reinforced by steel, was finally demolished with dynamite and the area was seeded over with grass.[4]

– Chapter Ten –

The Collection Points

One of the greatest problems facing the Allies at the end of the war in Europe had to do with the collection, sorting, and returning of European cultural objects to their countries of origin. These objects included works of art, gold, jewels, archives, and libraries—all of which were displaced as a direct result of World War II. To provide a means of organizing and processing these items, the United States established three main collection points in the U.S. zone of Germany.

Archival material books and precious scrolls, primarily looted from Jewish collections, were dispatched to the Offenbach Archival Depot. Offenbach eventually absorbed a grand total of 1,841,310 items and about three million books. The Wiesbaden Collection Point held mostly German works of art, primarily from former state museums, plus some loot seized from Germans after the war. Wiesbaden eventually held about 700,000 objects. The third site, the Munich Collection Point, specialized in art objects seized from museums as well as art taken from individuals. The Munich Collection Point contained over one million objects. These collection points contained approximately one-fifth of the artwork in the entire world. The transfer of valuable property to these collection points began immediately after the war.

The Offenbach Archival Depot

During the terror that was inflicted on the Jews during World War II, most of the sacred religious objects and books from Jewish Synagogues and museums had been stolen or destroyed by the Nazis from collections throughout Europe. This process began in the mid-1930s soon after the Nazi Party rose to power. "Prohibited" Jewish literature was removed from public libraries and bookstores. Between 1939 and 1945, all Jewish-related literature was confiscated from public and private libraries. Much of the looting took place in connection with the deportation of Jews to the notorious concentration camps.

A large warehouse in Offenbach, Germany, was selected by the American Army to reassemble the artistic heritage of the Jewish people, along with 2,859,418 books.[1]

The books were taken to the fifth floor warehouse at the Offenbach Depot, where they were sorted as to category.

Sorting rooms, like the one pictured on the left, were established to consolidate the books for shipment to their country of origin. These books are of Western origin.

The shipping room established for the return of books. It was the responsibility of the country of origin to pick up the books.

The catalog page shown below, created in the photography room at Offenbach, evidences a handful of selected library markings. This catalog, and others like it, are housed in the National Archives, OMGUS, Property Division, Box 779, Washington, D.C.

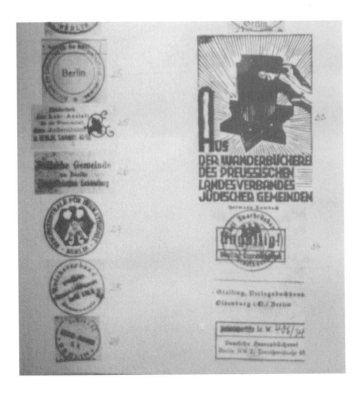

The Ex-Libris catalog (left) was created at the Offenbach Archival Depot. (Below Left) A page from the Ex-Libris catalog, featuring selected bookplates from the original owners. (Below) A bookplate once belonging to Paul Schlitte, who was obviously a member of the Nazi Party.

U.S. forces in Frankfurt, Germany, discovered 77,000 Hebrew and Yiddish publications jammed into a large building. This literature had been carefully collected and preserved by the Nazi Security Office (RSHA). It was slated to be housed in the Institute der NSDAP zur Erforschung des Judentums, a large library ostensibly

This large building in Frankfurt, Germany, was found to contain 77,000 stolen Hebrew and Yiddish publications.

organized to study Jewish culture. The Frankfurt collection contained the library of the Jewish Congregation of Berlin, the library of the Fraenkel Rabbi Seminary in Breslau, and many smaller synagogues. These tens of thousands of books were packed into 382 large cases and shipped to the Library of Congress in Washington, D.C.[2]

The final disposition policy of the items collected at the Offenbach Depot was a decision for the Department of State. On September 22, 1946, regulation WX-81072 clearly and unequivocally stated that objects removed by Germans from Jews or Jewish organizations or groups in formerly occupied countries should be returned to the country of origin. This restitution order was in accordance with Allied policy and, according to representatives of the Allies, the only just procedure to follow in regard to Jewish interests—regardless of the desires of some elements of American Jewry or other Jewish factions.

Because of the Holocaust in Europe, however, many displaced and homeless Jews who owned or were entitled to these valuables had immigrated to Palestine. They entered Palestine in violation of the British Mandate. As England's ally, the United States honored its request not to transfer Jewish Materials from Offenbach to Palestine, because it was unacceptable to the British Government to do so. (It should also be noted that Israel was not slated to become a country until May 14, 1949, under a mandate by the United Nations.)

In 1947, five cases of Jewish books and documents were sent to Jerusalem without authorization. The items were identified as belonging

to Russian museums, and Italian and Austrian citizens. One item belonged to Dr. Josef Breuer of New York City. This action generated "Top Secret" telegrams between the British General Council in Jerusalem and the U.S. Army in Germany. The telegrams requested the immediate return of the five boxes to Offenbach. In spite of intense political pressure, the boxes remained in Jerusalem.[3]

After the establishment of Israel, the remaining inventory of the Offenbach Archival Depot was shipped to Jerusalem in one large shipment and placed in the custody of Dr. I. Joel, Acting Librarian, Hebrew University. The agreement was signed on February 15, 1949, between the

The Jewish religious items (left and opposite page) were not returned to the country of origin because a committee representing leading Jewish organizations suggested that no restitution be made to governments of countries where Jewish communities had been substantially eliminated.

United States Military and the Jewish Restitution Successor Organization (JRSO), a New York-based agency acting as trustee for the Jewish people. The agreement held that JRSO would exercise reasonable diligence to locate the owners of this Jewish cultural property within two years and return the property to them. The rightful owner would be required to pay for shipment and insurance. If the owners could not be located within two years, the property was to be utilized for the maintenance of the cultural heritage of the Jewish people. The agreement further stated that ritual objects of precious metal could not be converted into monetary metal.[4] The Offenbach Depot was closed in June 1949, shortly after the last shipment to Israel.

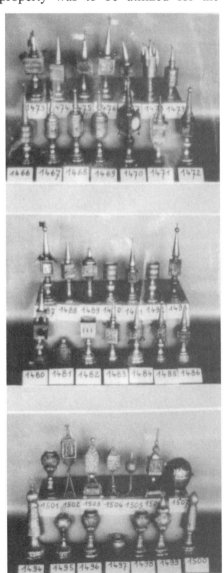

The Wiesbaden Collection Point

In July 1945, Captain Walter I. Farmer established the Wiesbaden Collection Point. The modern building he selected was built in 1920 as an art museum. During the war, the museum was taken over by the Luftwaffe. Shortly before the Wiesbaden collection point was established, the building was utilized for yet another purpose, this time by the U.S. 12th Army Group as a clothing warehouse.

Other than broken glass and some injury to the roof, the building had escaped serious structural damage during the war. Still, it took Farmer and his men two months to recondition the facility for its new task. The Wiesbaden depot was the major collection point for German-owned art. Valuable objects taken from the Kaiseroda, Ransback, Bernterode, and Grasleben mines were transferred to Wiesbaden from the Foreign Exchange Depository. The major portion of the holdings from two of the greatest museums in Germany, the Berlin and the Frankfurt museums, along with the scattered collections from many other places and individuals, were eventually housed here. Germany's most valuable art, still packed in the original and carefully labeled boxes, filled 75 of the 300 rooms of the Wiesbaden Collection Point.

One room, the so-called "Treasure Room," was kept under special guard. Inside its walls were pieces of art once owned by dukes, bishops and kings. The renowned Egyptian collection of the Berlin Museum, for example, was shipped from the Foreign Exchange Depository and upon arrival examined in its original five-by-five-foot box. The container was filled with glass wool packing, and wrapped in silk paper within was the famous sculptured head of Queen Nofretete (Nefertiti).

In 1933, shortly after Hitler came to power, Egypt made an offer to exchange Nofretete for an imposing sculpture of the Old Egyptian Empire. The Berlin museum officials agreed to the trade, but the Führer flatly refused to consent, claiming that the bust was not only his favorite, but one of the most outstanding and popular pieces of art in all of Germany. While Nofretete was at Wiesbaden, the Egyptians sued the Allies in an attempt to regain the 3,316 year-old bust, charging fraud on the part of the Germans. The claim was denied. Egypt was one of the few countries that did not see a return of looted art.[5]

Captain Farmer returned early to the United States, and his Wiesbaden Collection Point was placed under the command of Captain Edith Standen. Standen, whose father was

Some of the rooms at the Wiesbaden Collection Point, jammed with artwork.

The most sensational object at the Wiesebaden Collection Point was the bust of Nofretete (Nefertiti), Queen of Pharaoh Eohnathon. Germany's most celebrated art treasure was excavated in 1910 at Tell el Amarna by the German Oriental Society. The finds of the excavation were divided between the Egyptian and German governments, with Nofretete going to Berlin, causing at once a sensation there.

English and mother from Boston, was born in Canada but by 1945 was a naturalized American citizen. Educated in England, she later was in charge of the Joseph Widener Collection, the most noteworthy private collection of its period. When it was given to the National Gallery in 1942, Standen found herself out of a job and joined the Women Air Corps (WACs).[6]

One of the issues Standen oversaw at Wiesbaden was the shipment of 202 works of art—part of the collection of the German State's Kaiser Frederick Museum—to the United States. The most valuable paintings belonging to the German government were ordered sent to the National

Gallery of Art in Washington. General Lucius Clay originated the idea in July 1945 at the Potsdam Conference. President Harry S.

Captain Edith Standen

Edith Standen (far right), with Captain Rose Valland, French MFA&A officer, and a suit of armor. At the close of the war, all pieces of art stolen or otherwise acquired from other countries by Germany since 1933, as well as all weapons, were seized by the U. S. Military. This included suits of armor and antique weapons that had not been used for hundred years. The military law governing this issue was so precise that a sword-swallower from Karlsruhl had his 14 sabers confiscated—despite the fact they were only theatrical props.

Truman, believing the decision was a good one for the art world in general, agreed with Clay, and the order authorizing the transfer was made in four months later in November.

The officers overseeing the collection and distribution of the items in question felt betrayed by their own government, and the decision whipped up a storm of controversy. Twenty-four of the thirty-two officers signed a letter of protest. "No grievances will rankle so long, or be the cause of so much justified bitterness as the removal of the paintings," they wrote. The letter also pointed out that the Allies were at that very time prosecuting individuals who were claiming they acquired artwork and other items of value as a means of safekeeping it (i.e., protective custody). Alfred Rosenberg, on trial at Nuremberg, for example, used this as part of his defense. According to Rosenberg, he took collections into custody to protect them from the ravages of war. (Rosenberg was eventually hanged for his role as German minister for the occupied Eastern Territories.) How, argued the officers, can the United States justify confiscating the same items earlier taken by the victorious Germans? Many of the MFA&A officers requested transfers. Their argument held substantial merit. The art undeniably belonged to Germany, and German criticism against the removal was immediate and sharp. German staff members working at the collection points threatened to quit their jobs, and absolutely refused to participate in the transfer of the 202 pieces of art selected for shipment to the United States

The protests, however, fell on deaf ears, and preparations for the shipment—named, appropriately, "Westward Ho"—continued apace. The operation took precedence over all other activities at Wiesbaden. Lieutenant Lamont Moore was selected to direct the assignment. Under Moore's supervision, the Kaiser Frederick Museum pictures were selected and removed from the original cases they had been packed in for shipping from Berlin to Merkers. After the individual selection process was complete and the items repacked into their cases, the artwork was shipped in a special metal railway car to Le Havre, France. From there, the 45 cases were shipped on the *USS James Parker* to America. Lamont Moore accompanied the valuable cargo to the National Gallery in Washington, D.C., and assumed a job assignment with the gallery. Within the National Gallery, Moore worked with the American Commission for the Protection and Salvage of Artistic and Historical Monuments in War Areas.

The Munich Collection Point

On June 4, 1945, two naval officers, Lieutenants Craig Smyth and J. Hamilton Coulter, arrived in Munich to establish the what would come to be called the Munich Collection Point. Two building sites selected as

suitable for the task were the *Führerbau* and *Verwaltungsbau* near the Königsplatz. The Nazi Party had once used these twin

Boucher's *Mercury and Venus* (left) was one of the paintings shipped to the United States, together with 201 other similar and invaluable pieces.

Rubens' "Fall of the Damned" (left), was yet another priceless painting from the Kaiser Frederick Museum that wound up in the United States.

buildings as its headquarters. Instead of using the Nazi names for the buildings, however, they were referred to as simply Gallery I and Gallery II. The name change was in accord with an army directive to immediately remove all Nazi names from shrines, streets, memorials, parks, places, and buildings, all as part of the denazification process agreed upon by the allies.

After a sweep by a bomb squad—considerable German ammunition and hand grenades were found and removed from the building by German prisoners of war—repair work began on the damaged structures. Refuse was cleaned out of the galleries and large quantities of furniture were removed from storage rooms. Also removed by U.S. Military Intelligence was a large file containing the complete membership list of the Nazi Party, which helped the Allies track down party leaders and war criminals.

An electrical powerhouse building used to heat and provide electricity for the Nazi headquarters complex was refurbished and used for a separate German employee canteen. This separation was the results of an order by Eisenhower for all Americans to abstain from any social contact with Germans of any sex or age. The order prohibited visiting, drinking, eating, or even shaking hands with a German. This policy led to humorous interpretations, such as the standing joke that "copulation without conversation is not fraternization." It is a sad irony of the times

The *Verwaltungsbau* or Gallery I, was one of two buildings in the Königsplatz in Munich used to store the vast collection of art seized by the American Army.

that the segregated black U.S. Army truck drivers, who transported art objects for the collection point, were also housed in the same building.

Routine restitution of the art objects from the collection points began when large shipments were returned to France, Belgium, and the Netherlands. When agreements to ship art items were reached, the art officer overseeing the transfer made arrangements with a transportation company for shipment from the collection point, by train or truck, to the final destination. The responsibility of the United States ceased with the loading of the valuables. The acquiring country signed a receipt for the items. This receipt, in turn, made it the responsibility of the acquiring country to return the valuables to its own citizens. Problems of individual ownership were left to the governments concerned, leaving the Unites States free from any liability.[7]

In addition to returning valuables to their country of origin, large troves of these items (other than those from the Kaiser Frederick Museum) were shipped to the United States. The *Weltkriegsbücherei* (German World War Library), a privately endowed collection pertaining to World War I, was removed from the Kochendorf Salt Mine in April 1946 by MFA&A officials. The 80,000-book library was founded in 1915. Although its

The Munich Collection Point was more than a warehouse. It was the administrative headquarters and technical operating center for all monument and fine art activities, and contained a large research library, pictured above.

original purpose was to collect all publications relating to the history of the Great War, the library enlarged its focus to include 19th and 20th century German and foreign language books without regard to nationality and political creed. Ironically, this collection of books was established for historical research on the causes, events, and consequences of World War I, in order to learn from the past and safeguard

Art such as this self-portrait of Albrecht Dürer (left) and gold chain from Charles V (opposite page, top) were placed in separate national rooms for examination and for proof of identity from claimant countries.

humanity against a second catastrophe.

After its removal from the Kochendorf Salt Mine, the German World War Library was shipped to the Library of Congress in America. In 1947, Weltkriegsbücherei officials wrote several letters to MFA&A officer Captain Edith Standen, requesting its return. Standen, in turn, wrote Major L. K. Born, a MFA&A officer and later employee of the Library of Congress, the following:

> You will remember the letter I wrote not long before I left Stuttgart on the Weltkriegsbücherei. It seemed to me a great injustice had been done, and as I am spending a few days in Washington, I thought I would find out the present status of the library and the project for returning it. I got in touch with the Library of Congress and they showed me the list of material brought from Germany. The Weltkriegsbücherei, with others is noted as not unpacked pending a decision as to disposition not as "packed for return" like the Patent Library.
>
> Perhaps the feeling would be that the Germans should not be allowed to do research on the cause and cure of war. You know better than I, but I thought you would like to know what the situation is here, so that you can take the matter up again; if you feel justified in so doing.[8]

A large number of art objects taken to the Munich Collection Point were found at Neuschwanstein Castle in Füssen, Germany. The impressive fortress, built on top of a steep and rocky cliff, was one of many extravagant buildings erected by the eccentric King Ludwig II at the height of the 19th-century romantic revival. In the fall of 1945, Major Edward E. Adams was assigned the duty of evacuating the valuables discovered at Neuschwanstein.

Security guards and transportation were provided by French soldiers, who were garrisoned in the zone occupied by France, only eight miles from Neuschwanstein. This arrangement was especially appropriate since much of the loot found hidden at the castle had been stolen from their home country. Since it would take several days to load the cars, the French guards were stationed in two cabooses placed in strategic positions in the freight yard.

The first shipment consisted of 22 freight cars of art. Under the supervision of several assistants from the Munich Collection Point, German boys from a former naval cadet camp near the castle packed and crated the remaining material. Adams hired these workers, ages 14-18, as well as their teachers, to work for the Allies. All of them were glad to find whatever employment they could in postwar Germany. The loaded railcars at Neuschwanstein were numbered in sequence and painted with the letters "MFA" (Monuments and Fine Arts).

The cars containing French art were shipped immediately to Paris. In all, a total of 41 freight cars were loaded and dispatched. Once in France, the most precious pieces, such as those created by Boucher, Fragonard, and Regnault's *The Three Graces*, were immediately placed on display at the Jeu de Paume Museum.[9]

This image clearly shows the wide variety of valuables stored in orderly racks in locked rooms at the vast Neuschwanstein Castle.

Half of the items at Neuschwanstein Castle were still in the crates and identified as items originally shipped from Paris to Germany by the Nazi organization "Task Force Rosenberg." The decision was made to verify these crates as French in origin and, without unpacking and checking the individual objects, ship them directly to Paris.

Regnault's *The Three Graces* was one of the pieces of art immediately placed on display at the Jeu de Paume Museum in Paris, France.

Chapter Eleven

The Imperial Crown Jewels of the Holy Roman Empire

P erhaps the most prominent treasure to cross an international frontier during World War II was the Imperial Crown Jewels and Coronation Regalia of the Holy Roman Empire. These priceless objects dated from the 8th through the 14th centuries, and their history is full of interesting twists and turns.

During the second half of the 13th century, a decisive change in the monarchy system took place, and the Imperial Jewels were no longer considered to be at the free disposal of the king. As a result, these royal treasures were housed for long periods of time in numerous castles in Europe. After the death of Emperor Louis in the 14th century, the jewels were handed over to the new king, Charles IV, under condition that they remain permanently in Nuremberg. In 1424, the Imperial Jewels were delivered from Blindenberg castle near Budapest to Nuremberg "for all eternity."

Eternity came more quickly than anyone anticipated, and it arrived in the form of the French army, which approached Nuremberg in 1796. Nervous officials in Nuremberg decided to remove the royal accouterments, which were entrusted to the Diet of Austria-Hungary with the assurance that they would be returned to Nuremberg once the danger passed. It was in this manner and under these circumstances that the

Imperial Crown Jewels were deposited in the Court of Vienna. The threat eventually faded, but the jewels remained in Austria. In 1818, Nuremberg failed in its attempt to regain them. The city officials simply lacked the political muscle power and backing of higher government authorities. As a result, the Imperial Crown Jewels remained in Vienna for 142 years. And then the Nazis came.

On March 13, 1938, immediately after Germany's annexation of Austria, the Bürgermeister of Nuremberg, Willy Liebel, traveled to Berlin and received permission from Adolf Hitler for the return of the 32 pieces that comprised the Imperial Crown Jewels and Coronation Regalia. On the night of August 29, 1938, a specially equipped train escorted by a detachment of SS troops left the West Station of Vienna in absolute secrecy. The following day the treasure was transferred from the train to the temporary storage of St. Catherine's church in Nuremberg. Arthur Seyss-Inquart, the Austrian Reich Governor who would eventually be hanged for war crimes at Nuremberg, officially handed over the Imperial Regalia to Liebel. The jewels were exhibited in ten specially constructed glass cases and were accessible to the general public until 1940.

As the war in Europe intensified, the Imperial Jewels were carefully packed and stored in an air-conditioned air-raid shelter located beneath the Nuremberg Kaiserburg Castle. The bunker complex was 60 feet deep and carved out of solid rock. The Viet Stoss altarpiece was also stored here. This religious artifact is regarded by the Polish people as a national shrine comparable in significance to the Magna Carta or Liberty Bell. Viet Stoss, a native of Nuremberg, had been commissioned by the King of Poland in 1477 to carve this great work, which took ten years to complete. The Germans stole the priceless relic from the Church of Our Lady in Cracow, Poland, in April 1940, and sent it to Nuremberg.

On March 31, 1945, as the Allies advanced across Europe, Willy Liebel made sure the more valuable pieces—Holy Crown, Imperial sword, scepter, Imperial orb, and sword of St. Marice—were wrapped in fiberglass packing and soldered shut in four copper containers. The waterproof containers were walled up in the nearby Paniers Platz Bunker complex. The remaining 18 pieces of the Imperial Crown Jewels and Coronation Regalia remained in the deep chamber underneath the Nuremberg Kaiserburg Castle.

These well-traveled masterpieces remained intact until April 3, 1945. At that time, the five pieces walled up in the bunker were removed and, as reported by Bürgermeister Liebel, given to an SS colonel who drove away to an unknown destination. As the Americans advanced into Nuremberg, Liebel committed suicide (or possibly was murdered on the orders of the corrupt and sadistic Gauleiter of Nuremberg, Julius Streicher), because of an old grudge.[1]

When Nuremberg was captured on April 19, the 18 royal pieces stored beneath Kaiserburg castle were discovered by U.S. Forces and immediately secured by military personnel. It was not until two months later that authorities discovered the five most valuable pieces of the Imperial Crown Jewels and Coronation Regalia were missing. Many rumors circulated regarding their fate. One of them was that they had been sunk in the bottom of Zell am See. This gossip was attributed to SS Colonel Wilhelm Spacil, Financial Administrator of SS Security. Many believed Spacil was the SS officer who had removed the valuables in the first place.

On July 19, 1945, Lieutenant Walter W. Horn, professor of art at the University of California, was assigned the task of investigating the disappearance of some of the Imperial Jewels. Dr. Walter Fries, a Nuremberg official, had signed a sworn statement attesting that the SS had taken the valuables. Horn interrogated almost two dozen people at the Third Army Intelligence Center in Nuremberg without making any progress. Horn, who was aware of the rumor that the treasure was at the bottom of Zell am See, decided to confront Dr. Fries with Spacil, who was imprisoned at the Seventh Army Interrogation Center.

On August 3, Fries was arrested and spent the night in solitary confinement. Under the pressure of an interrogation and just prior to the scheduled confrontation with Spacil, Fries broke down. He confessed that his previous statements had been false, and a fictitious removal had been staged with the assistance of some local SS members to hide what really happened to the valuables. According to Fries, he was willing to reveal the location and assist in the recovery of the Imperial Jewels.

On the morning of August 7, 1945, Horn, Fries, and a small party of men met at the entrance of the Paniers Platz Bunker in downtown Nuremberg. The party descended deep into the bunker and then chiseled a hole through a brick wall into a small room. Four copper containers

The breathtaking Imperial Crown Jewels of the Holy Roman Empire, examined after their arrival in Austria by, left to right: Colonel Theo Paul, Andrew Richie, Commander Perry B. Cott, and Major Ernest T. Dewald.

were removed and taken to the air-raid shelter beneath Kaiserburg castle. When the containers were finally opened, the precious missing Imperial Jewels were found inside and in good condition. The Holy Crown, imperial sword, scepter, orb, and sword of St. Marice were unpacked from their spun glass enclosures and placed back in their original container, thus completing the collection of the Imperial Crown Jewels. Shortly thereafter, the Allies established Austrian ownership of the Imperial Crown Jewels.[2]

But the remarkable story of the Imperial Crown Jewels of the Holy Roman Empire does not end there. In January 1946, the Holy Crown, scepter, and orb turned up in Los Angeles, California! The valuables were acquired in Munich immediately after the war by U.S. Army Colonel Joseph W. Hensel. The FBI and U.S. Customs investigated the matter, which threatened an international incident. Photographs of the items were taken and dispatched to U.S. Army forces in Austria. On December 11, 1946, the vault of the National Bank in Vienna was opened and the Imperial Holy Crown, scepter, and orb were removed for comparison with the photographs. After considerable deliberation, Austrian officials concluded the items in the photographs were phony, and the genuine items were in their hands.

Eventually, Colonel Hensel donated the fake artifacts, valued at $15,000 (1945 value) to the U.S. Army. Today, the counterfeit Holy Crown, scepter, and orb are displayed in the National Infantry Museum, Fort Benning, Georgia.[3]

The Viet Stoss Altarpiece

The most important work of art returned to Poland after the end of World War II was the Viet Stoss Altarpiece. The return of the altarpiece was an event of some magnitude, one that served to lessen political tensions and heighten national pride.

The counterfeit Holy Crown, scepter, and orb are displayed in the National Infantry Museum, Fort Benning, Georgia.

(Right) The Viet Stoss Altarpiece in the Church of Our Lady, Cracow, Poland. The altar was the most valuable artifact returned to Poland after the end of World War II. Its return almost caused an international incident, and may have cost an American soldier his freedom—and his life.

A party of twenty-five people left Nuremberg on April 25, 1946, with the main escort traveling in Foreign Minister Joachim von Ribbentrop's former private railroad car, and thirteen U.S. Army enlisted men disbursed throughout the train for security. The altar, and everyone connected with it, became a focal point for demonstrations of solidarity and resistance against the occupying Soviet authorities and their repressive regime. As a result, the arrival of the prized altarpiece, together with the presence of the U.S. Military personnel, were an embarrassment to Polish authorities.

On May 5, the Polish Secret Police produced a .45-caliber bullet slug they claimed had wounded one of their agents. Several bloody

German workers and American guards at a railroad siding in Nuremberg, loading one of 27 carloads of valuable cargo for return to Cracow, Poland. Included was the most famous altarpiece in the world, the Viet Stoss Altar, looted by German Governor Hans Frank (hanged at Nuremberg for war crimes) after the invasion of Poland.

---

fights had taken place, and the party accompanying the return of the altar decided it was time to depart Cracow. The group assembled at the station and boarded a train, but Polish guards armed with rifles and machine guns arrived there as well with the clear intent of preventing the Americans from leaving. At about noon on May 6, developments reached a critical stage when the entire party was informed it

The portrait of Cecilia Gallerani, the so-called "Lady with a Weasel," by Leonardo da Vinci, was stolen from the Czartoryski Museum in Cracow by the Germans in 1939. It was returned, together with the Viet Stoss Altar and other Polish artifacts, by the U.S. Army as a gesture of democratic friendless. Their return coincided with Poland's National Independence Day.

was under arrest. The Polish Secret Police and two wounded Polish civilians identified Private Curtis Dagley as the soldier who had fired the shots. Dagley steadfast maintained his innocence and produced witnesses from among the guards to prove he was in his hotel at the time of the shooting. Dagley was not turned over to the Poles, and the U.S. delegation remained on the train.

That evening, Private Calvin L. Vivian entered the officers' car and announced he wished to confess to the shooting. The confession was taken down word for word by Captain Everett P. Lesley, Jr. The irate officers concocted a bold plan: Private Dagley would be given to the Polish police as the perpetrator of the shooting, thereby triggering the release the train for its return journey to the West. Private Vivian, meanwhile, would be put under arrest by the Americans and kept on the train. When the train arrived in U.S. occupied territory, Vivian's confession would be turned over to the Military Attaché of the U.S. Embassy, who would send a telegram to the U.S. Embassy in Warsaw informing them that the true culprit had been arrested, and demand the immediate release of Dagley.

Dagley was approached with the remarkable plan and, with great personal courage, agreed to the scheme. The train was released for its return journey to Nuremberg. Six months later, Dagley was still in prison. His final fate is unknown.[4]

Chapter Twelve

Saint Stephen's Crown

On November 7, 1944, as Russian armored divisions began encircling Budapest, Colonel Ernoe Pajtas, commander of the Royal Hungarian Guards, removed the Holy Crown and other coronation regalia from the Armor Room in the Royal Castle. He carried them safely to the branch office of the Hungarian National Bank in the town of Veszprem. On March 17, 1945, Colonel Pajtas, accompanied by twelve of the bank guards, loaded the Crown Jewels into a truck and drove them to Mattsee, Austria.

There, on the cold and clear night of March 26, Pajtas and two of his most trusted sergeants implemented their plan to protect the holy relics. They climbed into the truck and opened the large iron chest holding the artifacts and removed the Holy Crown, scepter, and sphere, all of which were still packed in their original leather coverings. Pajtas' hands must have trembled as he lifted out the priceless artifacts and carefully placed them into a military gasoline barrel that had been slit in half. Only the sword remained in the chest, which was quickly locked shut. Pajtas and the two sergeants took the bottom half of the barrel and carried it to the front of a sheer cliff, a remote location Pajtas had selected the day before. There, the men dug a deep hole, lowered the barrel into it, and covered it. Not a trace of their activity was visible. They had just buried one of the rarest treasures in the world.

(Left) Colonel Pajtas's mysterious chest. The iron container was locked with three padlocks (below), plus the built-in lock of the chest itself. The front bore the insignia of the Hungarian State: two angels carrying a crest.

To whom did these precious objects once belong? Saint Stephen I (1000-1038) was the first Hungarian Christian king. His goal was twofold: Christianize the pagan Hungarian tribes, who had migrated into Transylvania about 896 A.D. and establish an Hungarian state. Stephen believed

that his new Christian country would be welcomed by other Christian nations in Europe, and he was right. His actions solidified the future of Hungary until the present. For these lasting achievements he was given the title "apostolic king," and he was canonized in 1083, almost a half-century after his death.

On May 2, 1945, Colonel Pajtas and his guards drove to Zellhof, Austria, with the nearly empty chest still sitting in the back of the truck. They spent the next several nights in Zellhof in a Roman Catholic Mission House. On May 6, the Catholic priest of the mission went to Seeham, where an American command had been established, and told the Americans that a Hungarian colonel and a dozen enlisted men were at his monastery. At 5:00 p.m., a Lieutenant Granville jumped into his jeep and drove out to the monastery. The meeting between Granville and the Hungarians was cordial and to the point. Granville informed them that he was the son of the owner of a ladies garment store on Vaci Street in Budapest, and that they should surrender to him as American prisoners of war. Pajtas agreed that the time had come to surrender, but was concerned about the valuables still housed in the truck, which he refused to abandon—even for a moment. Granville agreed to allow Pajtas and his men to follow his jeep in the truck.

On May 7, the odd caravan led by an American lieutenant of Hungarian descent, whose prisoners included the commander of the Royal Hungarian Guards, his men, and the Hungarian royal sword, wound its way over 70 miles of road to Augsburg, Germany. There, the iron chest was delivered to Major Paul Kubala at the U.S. Seventh Army interrogation center.

One of the first questions put to Colonel Pajtas by Major Kubala had to do with the contents of the chest he was so zealously guarding. The chest, the colonel informed the shocked American officer, contained the Holy Crown of Saint Stephen and other coronation regalia. Since he was its custodian and guardian, continued Pajtas, it must remain within his sight at all times. Further questioning revealed that Pajtas did not have the keys to the iron treasure box.

The chest's alleged contents were of sufficient interest to the Americans to warrant further investigation. Kubala put Lieutenant Granville's Hungarian to good use for several weeks interrogating political prisoners, and on July 24, the keys to the chest finally turned up. Granville opened it in the presence of Major Kubala. Much to everyone's surprise (and perhaps disappointment), the chest contained only Saint Stephen's sword; the holy crown and other items were no where to be found. After another round of questions, Colonel Pajtas finally confessed that he knew the chest was empty all the time, and that he had personally removed the contents and buried them in accordance with his instructions as commander of the Royal Hungarian Guards

Pajtas's elaborate and prolonged prevarication put the U.S. Army in a rather delicate and potentially embarrassing position. It was common knowledge, explained Kubala, that the chest had been under the protection of the U.S. Seventh Army. Even President Harry Truman had been informed of the recovery of the Holy Crown. Now, Kubala was expected to show the historic relics to the president and to General Dwight D. Eisenhower. If he was unable to produce the artifacts, someone would have to explain why and where they were. Significant pressure was brought to bear against Pajtas, and he finally relented and shared his secret with Kubala: the crown and other relics were buried in Mattsee. Luckily for the Americans, that portion of Austria was then under the control of General George Patton's Third Army. Unfortunately for Major Kubala, this meant the Seventh Army Interrogation Center was not authorized to carry out a search in Mattsee. The mountain of red tape he would have to wade through just to search for the buried treasure annoyed Kubala to no end.

Lieutenant Worth B. Andrews of Fort Worth, Texas, an imaginative young soldier with a spirit for adventure, asked Kubala for permission to simply drive to Mattsee, dig up the crown and other items, and haul them out of the Third Army area. Kubala, however, was unwilling to take such a gamble with his career and declined the offer. Andrews, however, was not willing to abandon his plan. That night at 11:00 p.m., he woke Pajtas out of a dead sleep. "Come on, Colonel," Andrews drawled, "let's go and get the crown. Bring one of your men and also bring some weapons." Pajtas explained that as a prisoner, he had no weapons. Andrews left for a few minutes and returned with Sergeant Daniel H. Schoel. To Pajtas's surprise, the Texan handed pistols to him and one of his sergeants.

Next, Andrews knocked on Major Kubala's door and entered his room. Those standing outside later reported that a heated discussion took place, during which Kubala refused to allow his subordinate to drive to Mattsee to get the relics. The young Texan left Kubala's quarters and motioned for Pajtas, his sergeant, and Sergeant Schoel to follow him. The four men walked out into the dark night, put a jeep in neutral, and pushed the vehicle down the road a few hundred yards. When he was far enough away, Andrews started the engine and drove off for Austria in a jeep loaded with shovels and pickaxes.

In Munich, Andrews and company reached the demarcation line of the Third Army area. The sleepy guard on duty accepted Andrews' credentials without question and motioned the party through. It was still dark when they reached Mattsee. After two hours of nocturnal digging, they reached

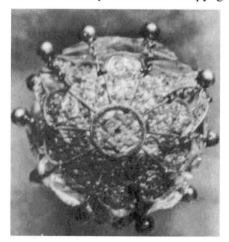

The head of the Royal Scepter, showing the ten little balls hanging from golden chains. They offer an attractive ringing sound when moved.

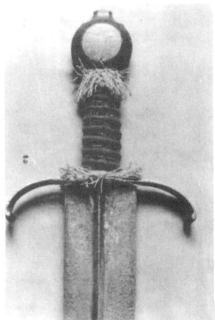

(Below) The fourteenth-century orb, a hollowed sphere of silver gilt with a dual cross-mounted on top and two coats-of-arms engraved in its sides representing the Hungarian Kingdom and the French-Italian dynasty. The orb, which symbolized kingly power and justice, and was kept in a velvet-lined wooden box.

(Above) The Sword of Saint Stephen symbolized the king's authority as supreme warlord. It was a straight sword, double-edged, with a regular taper. It was sheath-lined with red velvet and kept in a leather box.

the gasoline barrel containing the Holy Crown and related items. The artifacts were in good condition except for the leather coverings, which were showing signs of wear from their underground storage. All of the men silently admired the Holy Crown, which sparkled in the gleam of the jeep's headlights. By noon the next day, the four men

The gold, enameled, and bejeweled Holy Crown of Saint Stephen was housed in a velvet-lined wooden box inside the royal chest. It consists of two separate parts: the lower circular crown, known as the Greek crown (corona graeca), and the upper arch-type crown, called the Latin crown (corona latina).

were back at Seventh Army Interrogation Center with the old mud-covered gasoline drum, which they deposited in Major Paul Kubala's room. The stunned officer, who could hardly believe his eyes, embraced both his disobedient subordinate—who had cut through the red tape.

Colonel Pajtas opened the drum and removed three muddy and deteriorated leather-covered boxes. Kubala and Pajtas washed the mud and dirt off the items into the bathroom, placed them on the floor to dry, and packed them back in the original iron chest. The interior of the chest was lined with leather and the subdivided compartments now contained the following pieces: the bejeweled Holy Crown of Saint Stephen; the Royal Scepter, symbolizing royal power and justice; a 14th-century orb, representing the territory and soil of the kingdom; and the Sword of Saint Stephen, representing the eternal defense of the country.[1]

The crown, which is actually two separate crowns placed together, is especially lovely and enjoys a unique history. The lower circular Greek-style portion of the crown was crafted in 1074 by Emperor Michael Dukas of Constantinople (1061-1108), and given as a gift to the Hungarian King Geza I. On one of the separate golden geometric plates adorning the crown is the figure of Jesus Christ sitting on a throne, his right hand for blessing and his left holding a book. He is surrounded by archangels, Byzantine warriors, and saints. In front directly beneath the figure of Christ is a large Indian sapphire. Other jewels surround the crown, including garnets, another sapphire, pearls, and green glass. Four delicate gold chains, complete with gems dangling from the ends, hang from each side. The precious ornaments symbolized the water (sapphire), fire (garnet), and the earth (green glass), i.e., the entire world.

The older, or arched upper Latin-style portion of the Holy Crown, was given to Saint Stephen by Pope Sylvester II (circa 945 -1003) in 1000 A.D. in recognition of his success in spreading Christianity to the Hungarians, and also as a means of recognizing the new unified Hungarian state. Christ is again depicted, as are eight of his apostles. Golden ornamental wire, jewels, and pearls adorn it. At the very top of the arch is a small golden cross, bent slightly to one side, and not original to the crown. Many believe the original provided by Pope Sylvester II was a receptacle containing a fragment of the cross on which Christ was crucified. The two gifted crowns were first attached by Hungarian King Geza I near the end of the 11th century.

The Royal Scepter is also especially noteworthy. Unlike some royal scepters, Saint Stephen's looks as much like a mace as a symbol of royal power. Its head is made of a 2.75 inch crystal sphere carved with three crouching lions. (Some sources claim it is the third largest hole-drilled crystal in the world.) The crystal is held in place by three gold clamps covered with gilded silver wire woven in a fine and intricate fashion. The crystal is mounted on the top of a hazelwood handle festooned with a similar gilded silver wire pattern. Some historians believe the scepter came from 10th century Egypt and the reign of the Fatimida kings. On the top of the clamps holding the crystal sphere is a Byzantine-era "magic knot,"designed to keep away bad luck, as are the ten little balls hanging from golden chains which, when shaken, keep away evil spirits.[2]

During his stay at the Seventh Army Interrogation Center, Colonel Pajtas never revealed to Major Kubala why he had buried the Holy Crown, royal orb, and scepter—but maintained possession of the chest and sword. Why didn't Pajtas bury the complete chest and its contents? The reason rested with Ferenc Szalasi, the Nazi-appointed Prime Minister of Hungary. Knowing that the war was lost, Szalasi devised a plan to utilize the royal relics for his own ends. His scheme included Pajtas, who was to hide only the crown, orb, and scepter, and then make

The crown treasures and heirlooms that once belonged to the first king of Hungary, Saint Stephen, are in this iron chest. They were taken into custody by the U.S. Seventh Army and sent to Fort Knox, Kentucky, where they remained until President Jimmy Carter arranged for their return thirty-three years later.

Lieutenant General S. Leroy Irving and Dr. Andreas Rohracher, Prince Archbishop of Salzburg, meet in the cardinal's palace to discuss the return of the Hungarian Holy Crown and other Hungarian relics. At this time in 1945, neither man had any idea symbols of Hungarian nationhood—Saint Stephen's Crown and other Hungarian relics—would not be returned to their homeland for 33 years.

himself available to the Allies with only the locked chest and sword in his possession. The pair had planned to charge the Americans with the theft of Hungarian's royal artifacts. Szalasi had hopes of returning to Hungary in authority after the war. At a time calculated for maximum effect, he intended to "discover" the hiding place of the Holy Crown, and use the press coverage to turn himself into a hero in the eyes of the Hungarian people. Unfortunately, for Hungary, Szalasi's scheme almost ended up losing the crown jewels forever.[3]

Although high level meetings were held in 1945 discussing the return of the Saint Stephens treasures, the priceless artifacts were confiscated by United States authorities. When pressed about the sensitive matter, the State Department issued a statement in 1951 claiming that the United States did not consider the items as a "spoils of war," but stored them as a deposit. The Holy Crown, Scepter, Orb, and Sword were kept in Fort Knox, KY, until 1978, when they were finally returned to Hungary by the Carter Administration.

Chapter Thirteen

The Theft of the Hesse Crown Jewels

O ne of greatest robberies of all times was the theft of the Hesse Crown jewels, stolen after World War II from Kronberg castle by Major David Watson, Colonel Jack Durant, and his lover, Captain Kathleen Nash.

Kronberg castle had an interesting history. It was owned by 74-year-old Countess Margarethe Hesse, the Princess of Prussia and granddaughter of Queen Victoria of England. The Countess's mother, also named Victoria, had been empress of Germany during her husband's 100-day reign, and was also the mother of Germany's Kaiser Wilhelm II. It was during this regime that Victoria had the picturesque medieval Kronberg Castle constructed nine miles northeast of Frankfurt, Germany.

The German Hesse family had ruled the Province of Hesse, which consisted of 8,000 square miles and a population of 4.5 million people, from the Middle Ages until 1918. Kronberg castle was a part of the House of Hesse, an enterprise that owned and managed land, houses, jewels, and other property. These valuable tiaras, hundreds of platinum necklaces with pearls, rubies and diamonds, gold broaches with sapphires and diamonds, and hundreds of other jewels, were purchased or inherited over the years from English, Greek, and Italian royal families. These possessions—known to some as the Landgrafin and Kurhesse jewels—were collectively called the Hesse Crown Jewels.

The 17th-century Kronberg Castle was the scene of one of the most opulent robberies of World War II—the theft of the Hesse Crown Jewels.

The director of the House of Hesse was Philipp von Hesse, a descendent of Emperor Friedrich III of Prussia. In 1925 he married Princess Mafalda, second daughter of King Victor Emmanuel III of Italy. Philipp maintained close contacts with Benito Mussolini, the fascist Italian dictator, and other the ruling Italians authorities. It seems as though Phillip was aware of Mussolini impending arrest in Italy in 1943 and consequent fall from power—but did not notify Hitler. In retaliation, on September 8, 1943, Phillip and his wife, Princess Mafalda, were arrested without warning and sent to Buchenwald Concentration Camp. There, the princess was forced into prostitution and suffered unspeakable suffering. Used as a human shield and chained to a nearby defense factory, her arm was severed by Allied bombs and she bled to death.

Kronberg castle was requisitioned after the cessation of hostilities as a country club for U.S. Army Officers, and Captain Kathleen Nash was appointed hostess of the officer's club. In November 1945, Captain Nash and her staff were exploring the castle when they discovered a fresh patch of concrete down in far corner of the cellar. Obviously, someone had been working on the floor recently. Had something been buried there? Nash and her friends left and returned with a hammer, chisel and shovel, and began chipping away at the concrete.

The primary instigator of the theft, Captain Kathleen Nash, divorced her high school sweetheart, left her two 19-year children, subtracted nine years from her age and joined the army as a 30-year-old "to get away from it all."

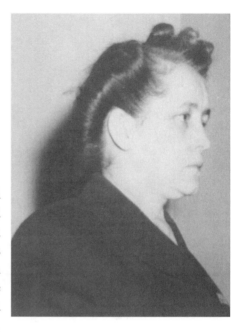

Before long, a zinc-lined chamber was uncovered, and within it was a wooden box containing several packages individually wrapped in brown paper. Inside was hidden the Hesse Crown Jewels, a collection of necklaces, crowns, and other jewelry worth millions of dollars. It is not difficult to imagine the shock that must have swept over Watson, Durant, and Nash, when they realized what they had just uncovered.

Instead of turning in the jewels, however, they decided to steal them. The trio removed the diamonds and other gems by pushing them from their settings or cutting them loose from the various tiaras, necklaces, and bracelets; the gold settings were quietly sold in Switzerland.

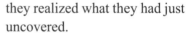

A fortune in jewels and other valuables were chiseled from this zinc-lined box embedded in the concrete cellar of Kronberg castle.

The jewels pictured on this page were stolen by Major David Watson, Colonel Jack Durant, and his lover Captain Kathleen Nash. The diamonds, emeralds, pearls, and sapphires were removed from their settings, and the gold was sold in Switzerland. The larger gems disappeared from a parcel checkroom in the La Salle Train Station in Chicago, and have never been recovered.

(Above) Princess Margarethe, the Landgrafin of Hesse and Granddaughter of Queen Victoria of England. (Below) Princess Sophia of Hanover, daughter of the King of Greece.

Princess Mafalda, daughter of the King and Queen of Italy. She was sent to Buchenwald Concentration Camp and forced into prostitution. Used as a human shield, chained to a nearby defense factory, her arm was severed by Allied bombing and she bled to death.

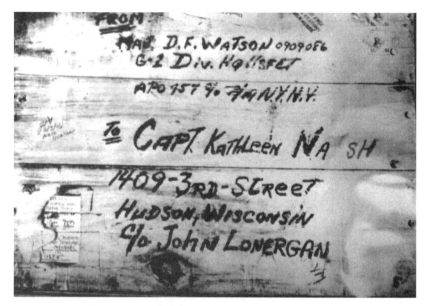

Major David Watson shipped the bulk of the "small stuff" from Germany to the home of Nash's sister in Hudson, Wisconsin.

The three looters returned to the United States in late 1945 and smuggled many of the valuables into the country with them. In addition to the jewels and gold, the thieves had also looted books, silverware, dishes, and other hundreds of other items. In January 1946, a member of the Hesse family reported the missing jewels to the U.S. Army. Investigations by the Army's Criminal Intelligence Division determined the magnitude of the thefts, and Watson, Durant, and Nash were quickly arrested. The Army's effort to recover the stolen jewels was swift and relentless. Half of them were recovered at the home of Nash's sister. Further inquiry revealed that the bulk of the outstanding jewels had reached the hands of organized criminal elements in Chicago. These larger and more valuable jewels were never recovered.

The primary instigator of the theft, Captain Kathleen Nash, had divorced her high school sweetheart, left her two 19-year-old children, subtracted nine years from her age and joined the army as a 30-year-old "to get away from it all." Ending up in a jail cell was not what she had in mind. Colonel Jack Durant, Captain Kathleen Nash, and Major David Watson were court-martialed in 1946. Durant married Nash so that she

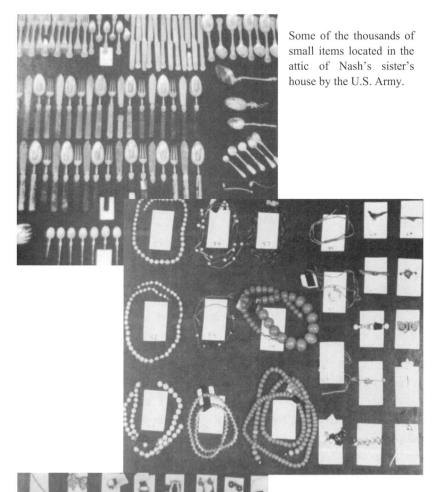

Some of the thousands of small items located in the attic of Nash's sister's house by the U.S. Army.

would not be able to testify against him. At trial, the three accused offered the defense that looting and souvenir hunting was common in Germany, and as a result, their misconduct should be excused. This pathetic defense did not hold much water with the court members. Nash

A small portion of the jewelry stolen from Kronberg castle. The bulk of the valuable jewels were never recovered.

was sentenced to five years in prison and Durant got 15 years. Watson received three years. Durant served about six years and was released on February 18, 1952. Nash, however, was a troublesome prisoner. She served her full sentence and then some, and was released after Durant on November 6, 1952. The couple remained married, and both later died of apparent alcoholism. Watson served only four months before he was released. His family owned a large grocery store chain on the west coast, and it is likely they cashed in their economic clout for legal leverage.[1]

The U.S. Army publically exhibited the valuables they recovered. When asked how much of the jewelry was mailed to her sister's house, Nash responded in a sworn statement, "Why, I think I probably have about one-half of it. I mean the small stuff." Under heavy guard valuables were heaped onto a table draped with a black cloth. Eye-blinding in brilliance, the display included four handfuls of cut diamonds. A pile of rough-cut emeralds was surrounded by a double handful of pearls. A line of diamonds and ruby bracelets valued at least at $25,000 bisected the table. One diamond wristwatch glittered with so many gems it was difficult to see the time-telling hands. There were also miniatures of porcelain, a host of trinkets, and a diamond ring with 12 carats.[2]

But what of the larger diamonds, rubies, and emeralds that had once bespeckled some of the most lovely crowns and necklaces ever created? To this day, no one knows their whereabouts.

Chapter Fourteen

German War Art

I n the fall of 1945, Captain Gordon W. Gilkey arrived in Germany. Captain Gilkey was in the Army Air Force and his assignment was to seize all "collections of art relating or dedicated to the perpetuation of Nazism." The captain interpreted this Military Government Regulation, Title 18, to include all works of art created by any member of the Nazi party, and carte blanche to take into custody most works of art created by any German during the 20th-century.

Gilkey's search for this art took on the characteristics of a massive treasure hunt. The paintings and sketches were scattered during the last chaotic days of the Third Reich. From Munich, Gilkey traveled to Alt Aussee and recovered part of this collection from salt bins in the salt refining plant there. These paintings were returned to Munich and more paintings were recovered from a bar, attics, and the basement of the House of German Art in Munich. Most of these German war art paintings were in the basement of Gallery I, previously known as the Führerbau, which had been the exhibit hall for the artwork.

Recognizing the importance of art as an instrument of spreading the Nazi doctrine of military superiority, Hitler established an art unit consisting of some eighty outstanding German artists. The art program was established after Hitler saw some remarkable paintings prepared during their leisure time by front line soldiers. The war artists were sent out to various fronts during the war where they completed sketches of front line scenes and action. This gave the paintings a look of

authenticity. Later, the German artists returned to the Army studios in the rear areas and with the proper materials, they turned out a wealth of art depicting the action of the German Armed Forces on all fronts. It was this art Gilkey was ordered to seize.

Captain Gilkey, in his words, "embarked upon a rigorous schedule to get the war art in some semblance of order. I became a recluse. I put in

These untitled oil paintings (above and opposite page, top) are housed in the Center of Military History in downtown Washington DC. According to the author, it almost took an "act of Congress" to see and photograph them.

14 to 15 hours daily and worked seven days a week until shipment of the pictures."

Three of the paintings found by Gilkey at Wiesbaden were small, neatly framed WWI-era watercolors by Adolf Hitler. The paintings of a railway embankment, a shelled Belgium village, and a courtyard in Munich, demonstrated Hitler's architectural abilities. His work, while good, hardly classified as fine art. Nevertheless, the three paintings have a high historical value (about $1,000,000).

The indefatigable Gilkey collected, labeled, and shipped to the United States more than 9,000 paintings. By March 1947, these paintings were housed in the Pentagon by the U.S. Historical Properties Section, U.S. Army. Many of them have nothing to do with the war or the Nazi Party, depicting instead outdoor scenes with woods, meadows, and animals. Many of the "war art" paintings and drawings are, however, brilliant in concept and execution. They show by their artistry, color, and mood the spirit of combat, and the desolation and tragedy of war. They are a testament to the sensitivity of the artist, regardless of the national origin.[1]

One of the paintings that ended up in the United States was wrapped in personal tragedy. In 1943, during the height of the war, Ludwig Orth

Wilhelm Wessel painted the above German officer while serving with Erwin Rommel in North Africa. Wessel, like Orth, tried in vain to have some of his art returned. He died in 1971; his art remained in the custody of the U.S. Army.

was surprised by a visit from one of his former students. The student was a member of the notorious SS, and was on leave from the Russian front. Having recently been promoted to captain and decorated with the Iron Cross 2nd Class, the young soldier asked his former professor to paint his portrait. The sympathetic Orth complied with the request. The young SS officer returned to the Russian front and was killed soon thereafter. The painting, entitled *SS Man*, was one of the paintings confiscated from the Haus der Deutschen Kunst by Captain Gilkey.

Ludwig Orth made every attempt to have the painting returned to his possession. In 1958, more than a decade after it was seized, Orth wrote a member of Congress to pleaded for the artwork."I did all I could in order to get back my portrait that had been declared as unsalable and that glorified in no way militarism. It only represented a pupil that was

SS Man, painted by the German war artist Ludwig Orth.

educated by me and fell in Russia as a soldier." Orth's plea fell on deaf ears. *SS Man* today resides in the basement of the U.S. Army Center of Military History in downtown Washington, D.C.

In 1981, the 97th Congress passed a bill authorizing the secretary of the army to return the paintings seized by Gordon Gilkey. Over the past twenty years, about one-third of the painting have been returned, leaving 6,342 pieces still in the hands of the army. The Air Force had acquired 563 pieces depicting various aircraft and combat scenes involving aircraft. Some of these paintings are on display today at the Wright-Patterson Museum. The bulk of the paintings were returned to Germany, but the Center of Military History selected the finest 400 pieces and kept them for its collection.

Chapter Fifteen

The Pillage of the Fabulous Horses of Europe

I n 1580, Archduke Carl of Austria opened a stud farm in the village of Lipizza near Trieste, with mares and stallions bought in Spain for the principal purpose of supplying the Austrian court with high-blooded riding horses. The horses bred and raised on the Imperial Austrian stud farm at Lipizza developed the magnificent breed we know today as Lipizzaner.

The Lipizzaner, famous and known by all horsemen through its use at the former Imperial Austrian court and the Spanish Riding School at Vienna, is today the only remaining breed of the former Spanish horse. A new breed was developed in Spain during the 700-year occupation by the Moors through crossbreeding the native Andalusian Spanish stock with Arab-Berber blood. This Spanish horse was as important to horse breeding in the Europe of the 14th-16th century as it is today in raising English thoroughbreds.

An integral part of the Austrian court had always been, since the 16th century, the rather oddly named "Spanish Riding School" of Vienna, which received its horses (stallions only) from Lipizza. The main function of this school was, and is still today, to maintain, preserve, and instruct in the classic art of horsemanship in its highest form. Stallions that had proven themselves at the Riding School through their character, forcefulness, and temperament were return to the stud farm at Lipizza for

Nordlicht (Northern Lights), shown here during an inspection by Kentucky Colonel Louie Beard and Colonel Fred L. Hamilton, was considered by many to be the finest horse in the world. This superb five-year-old stallion was seized from the Erhlendof stables near Frankfurt, Germany, and taken back to the United States for breeding purposes. Nordlicht, one of 143 horses captured in Europe, was the key attraction at the Parade of Horses and was considered so valuable as to be priceless. Chestnut in color, he stood 16 hands high and weighed 1,050 pounds.

breeding purposes. Stallions from six different families and mares from eighteen different families of the Iberian horse formed the basis of the horse breeding at Lipizza, which made it possible to overcome—in spite of the many years the Lipizza stud has been in existence—the dangers of inbreeding. Originally the studs at Lipizza served only the purpose of furnishing full-blooded horses for the Imperial Austrian Court. It was only a matter of time, however, before the magnificent Lipizzaner gained a considerable influence in the general horse breeding of the Austrian Empire.

After Germany occupied Austria in 1938, the Spanish Riding School at Vienna was permitted to function in its original form without much outside interference from the occupying forces. Between 1941 and 1943, all the Lipizzaner horses from the stud farms of Piber, Lipizza, and Demir Kapia were shipped to a central German stud farm at Hostau in Czechoslovakia. In early 1945, plans were formulated by the Germans to move the horses of the Spanish Riding School from Vienna to the northern part of Germany. At the insistence of the school's director, however, and only after considerable difficulties, the seventy stallions from the riding school were shipped to a private estate at St. Martin near Ried, in northern Austria.

It was at St. Martin that General George Patton and Secretary of War Patterson attended a performance of the Spanish Riding School on May 7, 1945. The display so impressed the general that he declared publicly that the school would be put under the protection of the American Army. Patton, who appreciated horses, must have realized that the Spanish Riding School and the Lipizzaner Stud were inseparable components; each needed the other. He ordered the removal of the Lipizzaner horses still remaining at Hostau to St. Martin, where they arrived at the end of May 1945.[1]

During the closing days of the war, Patton's Third Army, in its swift advance across Germany, captured several German army horse breeding farms and with them, several thousand valuable horses. In August of 1945, Patton returned to Washington for a brief visit. He had a long talk about the horses with Colonel Fred L. Hamilton, chief of the U.S. Army Remount Branch. After the conversation, Colonel Hamilton issued orders authorizing him to proceed to the American Zone, select, and

Four captured Lipizzaners from the Spanish riding school at Vienna draw a carriage around the show ring during the Army's exhibition of German horses at Front Royal, Virginia. In 1995, the bloodline of these proud Lipizzaners was shipped from Camp Pendleton, California, to Fort Myer, Virginia. Today, these spirited animals are being trained to pull caissons at Arlington National Cemetery.

return to the United States with as much equestrian stock as he felt would be of value to the U.S. Army horse breeding program.

Colonel Hamilton flew to Frankfurt and had six officers assigned to him, including two veterinarians. He then traveled to Altefeld, which had been established as a breeding farm in 1934 by the German army. The Germans assembled here such famous stallions as Brantome, Antonym, and many others, plus a large number of superior mares from all over Europe. Not only was the best stock of horses established at Altefeld, but the best horsemen and veterinarians were in charge of the horse farm. The farm had remained intact throughout the war, and in September 1945, was still a well-run complex with its original personnel.

The Germans tried to protect their best stock by hiding the most valuable breeding stallion in a remote shed. After some preliminary investigation and bribes in the form of cigarettes, a groom trotted out the magnificent chestnut thoroughbred. A German veterinarian, with a disgusted look on his face, muttered, "Well, you have the best now. That is Nordlicht, the finest horse in Europe." Colonel Hamilton agreed with the assessment, commenting, "This one horse alone would have been worth all the trouble and expense."[2]

Colonel Hamilton next visited Monsbach and Donnauworth, where some of the best German stock was found, as well as outstanding stock captured in Poland and many of the horses from the Hungarian State Stud Farm at Babolna. After more than a month of looking at horses, the colonel selected 152 of the animals for shipment to the United States. The horses consisted of 64 thoroughbreds, 40 half-breeds, 23 Arabians, 15 Arab Kinds, nine Lipizzaners, and one Russian horse.

The Germans had taken the thoroughbreds from the stables of the Aga Khan, Lord Derby, and Baron Edouard Rothschild. The half-breeds were selected after they were tested. Only horses that could run thirty-four miles in one hour and fifty minutes carrying 200 pounds—an almost impossible feat—were selected. The Lipizzaners had a stud book going back to 1558, and the Arab Kind came from Hungary and had maintained their original Arabian characteristics with a pedigree extending back to the early 1800s.

The horses were assembled and shipped to the port of Bremerhaven and then loaded aboard the liberty ship *Stephen Austin*. Stalls were rigged by nailing boards across the ends to contain the horses in the hold of the

These four two-year-old stallions drew the admiration of the crowd of nearly 10,000 horse lovers. A well-known horse breeder offered $250,000 for any one of the horses.

ship. Within a few days the ship was slammed with one of the North Atlantic's powerful storms. For thirty hours the *Stephen Austin* battled high winds and waves the size of small mountains. On one occasion, several of the horses were thrown completely out of their stalls and onto the deck of the ship into one large heap. Falling timber, kicking hooves, and iron bulkheads were tearing apart a fortune in horseflesh. The once beautiful animals offered up a sad sight when the ship finally docked at Newport News, Virginia, in October 1945.

The weakened horses were unloaded and shipped by rail, according to Patton's orders, to the quartermaster depot in Front Royal, Virginia. During the winter the horses were treated, conditioned, and nursed back to health. They were not shown to the public until April 7, 1946, at which time they were billed as "the finest horses in the world." At that time an exhibition was held before a crowd of several thousand visitors, including some of the best-known and most distinguished horse breeders in the United States. One of the guests offered $300,000 for the purchase of Nordlicht, an outstanding five-year-old stallion seized from the Erhlendof stables near Frankfurt, Germany. According to Mackey Smith, a writer for the horse breeder's magazine *The Chronicle*, Nordlicht "is the cream of French, German, and Hungarian blood stock. Nordlicht is one of the finest young sire prospects in the world." The breeders were notified

German Prisoners of War were grooms for the captured horses.

that in accordance with the army horse-breeding plan, all the horses would be offered to the public for a stud fee of exactly $10.

After the exhibition, the Arabian and Lipizzaners were sent to Pomona, California, the half-breeds to Fort Reno, Oklahoma, and the thoroughbreds divided between Front Royal and Robinson, Nebraska. The Army was busy making plans to add to the original contingent by bringing an additional 300 horses from the famous European stables. Many questioned the legality of this seizure under international law. The United Sates State Department, however, ruled that if the horses were properly appraised and entered on the books as inter-Allied reparations, the determination of the title would be settled internationally.

Legal or not, moral or otherwise, the widespread acquisition of these animals provided the American people what one German veterinarian described as the "finest horses in the world."[3]

– Chapter Sixteen –

The Return of the Hersbruck Soldiers

O n May 29, 1958, the last German soldiers captured and held by the Americans returned home to Hersbruck, Germany. During the demilitarization of Germany, 50,000 soldiers were captured and sent away into captivity. No one heard from or about them again for more than a decade. Finally, after years of investigation, 22,664 of these soldiers were found—many in the basement of a U.S. government building! The return of these warriors to their homeland was carried out without any fanfare as a result of the State Department's policy to maintain a low-key regarding returning POWs. These soldiers, who had been consigned to oblivion for so long, were actually valuable hand-painted and handmade two-inch tin warriors confiscated at the end of the war by U.S. Army officers. Their thirteen-year odyssey was finally over.

Their trip began in May 1945, when an American colonel, lieutenant, and three soldiers drove up to the Hersbruck Museum, marched in, and packed up the whole collection in wooden boxes they had brought with them for that purpose. The collection consisted of 500 regiments comprising 50,000 soldiers, including 6,000 on horseback and 1,200 regimental flags. Museum officials, outraged that the Americans were about to steal their most prized display, howled in protest. The tin soldiers, they were told, might be used by the Germans in the future for

The Hersbruck Soldiers (on this and the opposite page) on maneuver--prior to their capture by the U.S. Army.

dangerous military training purposes, and thus were subject to confiscation on the order of the Military Government in Ansbach!

As the years passed and tensions cooled, Hersbruck museum officials began searching in earnest for the missing soldiers. In 1952, they wrote to American officials in Germany, the State Department in Washington, D.C., and even the President of the United States. Each agency shrugged off the inquiries by claiming it did not have jurisdiction over the matter. An additional letter to President Eisenhower in 1955 was leaked to the press and made the newspapers. With the matter now squarely before the public, the Army began an investigation into the missing tin soldiers. Four hundred and twenty three tin warriors that had been requisitioned by an individual at Fort Sam Houston, Texas, were quickly discovered and turned over to the Army, which soon thereafter located 20,114 more in New York, and an additional 2,127 in Massachusetts.

Almost 23,000 soldiers had been returned. But what of the remaining 27,000 "prisoners" still missing? Nothing about their whereabouts could be found. In a letter dated January 5, 1961, Rudolf Wetzer of the Hersbruck Museum raised an interesting question: why were the tin soldiers illustrated in a newspaper photograph by the National Art Gallery not returned to Germany? A satisfactory answer was never forthcoming. According to the United States government, no further action was contemplated, and the investigation was concluded.[1]

The fate of the missing tin soldiers is still a mystery. Perhaps they are stored in some dark, back corner of a large government depot, or buried away and long forgotten in someone's attic.

Or, just perhaps, they are still on maneuver, changing formations, charging the enemy, and defending a position—in the hands of young children who have no idea of the value or history of the small tin soldiers that make up their playtime collection.

Chapter Seventeen

The Heinrich Hoffmann Photograph Collection

Henrich Hoffmann was an photographer with a strong propensity for alcohol. Although he had dismal luck with the bottle, his fortunes rose dramatically when he introduced Adolf Hitler to Eva Braun, who was then working as a clerk in his studio. Thereafter Hoffmann rose in Nazi party circles to become Hitler's photographer, first on a personal basis and later in an official capacity. He was present during all the early struggles of the Nazi Party.

After the rise of the Nazi party and during World War II, Hoffmann played a prominent political role by serving as the party patron of the modern art that flourished in Germany. Officially, he played a leading role in the campaign against what Hitler labeled "degenerate art," and under Hoffman's orders an attempt was made to remove all traces of it from German museums. The yearly exhibitions at the House of German Art in Munich, *Haus der Deutschen Kunst*, were under his direction.

In addition to his alcoholic nature, Hoffmann frequented the homosexual circles of Munich and Berlin. Against this backdrop, he met 25-year-old Erna Groebke, a lesbian who caused quite a stir by wearing men's breeches and a monocle. On at least one occasion at a popular nightclub, she picked up a female and attempt to join Hitler's table. There was considerable opposition to this from both Hitler and his guests. The

Henrich Hoffmann's Munich office. It was here that Adolf Hitler met Eva Braun, his mistress. At the height of the Nazi success, Hoffmann had offices in Berlin, Vienna, Munich, Paris, Strasbourg, The Hague, and Riga.

Führer let it be known that she would not be allowed to join the table under any pretext.[1]

Hoffmann's chief interest in the Nazi Party movement came, pure and simple, from the enormous amount of money he made from its success. He had a virtual monopoly on all photographic reproductions in Germany and, in particular, any picture having to do with any activity of the Nazi Party. Hoffmann's photographic creations were famous throughout Europe, and his market expanded with the victorious German armies. At the end of the war in 1945, Heinrich Hoffmann shipped his vast photographic and document collections from major European cities to his Castle Weinhöring, located west of Munich near to the Austrian border.

On May 6, 1945, the U.S. 13th Armored Division crossed the Inns River at Neuötting, Germany. Lt. Colonel William F. Malone, commander of the 59th Armored Infantry Battalion, ordered Lieutenant Orville Wells Martin and Sergeant Richard Kiekly to examine Weinhöring. The men were searching for a new and larger company headquarters, having outgrown their current quarters in a small hotel in

A wedding party for Eva Braun's friend, Marion Schönemann, during the halcyon days of the 1930s. Guests include (far left to right, standing), photographer Heinrich Hoffmann, Honni Morell, Erna Hoffmann, and Eva Braun. On the far right stands Adolf Hitler.

the town. After passing by an unfriendly field worker, the pair were welcomed into the castle by an unknown individual and encouraged to take a look around. Martin walked through the castle and decided that it was appropriate for their use. With the exception of a large ballroom, all of the rooms were basically empty.

Later, as Malone and Kiekly began examining the ballroom more closely, they found it was piled virtually to the ceiling with bales of medical supplies. They began clearing the room by throwing the supplies out of the large windows. They soon discovered the large bales were masking a cache of photographs in filing cases stretching from wall-to-wall and floor-to-ceiling. The cases were jammed with glass plates, prints, and 35mm negatives. Although they did not know it at the time, Martin and Kiekly had just uncovered the Hoffmann photographic collection, which contained more than 1,500,000 items. In addition to the photos, however, Hoffman's collection included a large cache of uniforms, ceremonial daggers, other miscellaneous military items—and four watercolor paintings by Adolf Hitler given to Hoffmann in 1936 by the Führer. The gigantic mass of photographs and other miscellaneous

Hitler put Hoffmann in charge of presenting the "right" art to the people of the Third Reich. The paintings on this page were included in the 1943 House of German Art exhibition.

items was removed from the castle and shipped to the Munich Collection Point.[2]

Because of his high ranking position within the Nazi Party and close affiliation with Hitler, Hoffmann was arrested. On March 6, 1946, he was convicted by a German Denazification Court for both publishing anti-Semitic literature and copyright infringement—Hoffman provided a Mickey Mouse which was used for nose art on a German plane!) All of his property except for 5,000 marks (or $1,190)

The author, standing beside two of Hitler's watercolor paintings that today hang in the U.S. Army's Military History Center in downtown Washington, D.C.

was confiscated, and he was sentenced to serve ten years in prison. It was reported that as Hoffmann left the courthouse, his young third wife, an Austrian woman named Anna Maria Kaspar, yelled "Heil, Moscow!" as their two children, ages seven and four, looked on.

The United States took advantage of the German decision and seized Hoffmann's photo and art collection. Hoffmann's son from his first marriage, Heinrich Jr., born October 24, 1916, strongly protested the U.S. action. The younger Hoffman claimed his father had given him the photos as a gift on his 21st birthday in 1937; therefore he, and not his father, was the owner in 1945. A cursory investigation by the U.S. Army quickly uncovered a number of contractual arrangements between the senior Hoffmann, other firms, and the German government, years after the collection had supposedly been given to Hoffmann's son. In other words, Hoffmann had still been in control of his collection when it was seized by the U.S. Army. On October 26, 1950, sixty-six large boxes comprising the Hoffmann collection were shipped to the adjutant general's office, King and Union Streets, in Alexandria, Virginia. The bulk of these materials ended up in the National Archives and Carlisle Barracks.

Heinrich Hoffmann died on December 16, 1957, and title to his property passed to his older son Heinrich Hoffmann, Jr., who in 1971 visited the United States and viewed the large Hoffmann photograph collection now stored in the National Archives.

In 1982, Billy Price, an oilman and noted Texas collector of valuable Nazi paintings, traveled to Germany and met with Hoffmann and his sister, Henriette von Schirach. Price showed them an army brochure containing the four watercolors painted by Hitler and presented to their father in 1936. Hoffman and his sister had been unaware that the originals were in U.S. hands. Later, they petitioned for the paintings to be returned. The U.S. denied the request.

Price, along with Hoffmann and his sister, filed a lawsuit against the United States government in 1984. Price agreed to fund the suit in exchange for two of the four Hitler watercolor paintings. After eleven years of litigation, the case defended by the federal lawyers broke down, and they were unable to successfully contest the Hoffmann children's right and title to their father's collections. The four Hitler watercolors and 1.5 million photos, however, remained in the United States. In September 1995, the U.S. government offered to pay Billy Price $8,000,000 plus court costs to drop his request for the return of the Hoffmann property. Price, who has criticized the government's efforts to drag out the case, commented, "Two judges have died on this case, the court reporter is dead, and all the plaintiffs except me are dead."[3]

As of the date of this writing, the lawsuit was ongoing.

Chapter Eighteen

Theft of the Quedlinburg Church Treasure

O
n June 14, 1990, the *New York Times* ran a front page article by William H. Honan titled, "A Trove of Medieval Art Turns Up in Texas." In an amazing discovery, wrote Honan, "a hoard of medieval artworks and illuminated manuscripts missing since they disappeared from an ancient castle town in Germany in the final weeks of World War II appear to have surfaced in this small farm town [Whitewright] in north central Texas, 15 miles from the Oklahoma border." The priceless items found in Texas were the subject of one of the world's greatest art thefts. Now, after the passage of almost half a century, the lingering mystery of what happened to the Quedlinburg Church Treasure had been solved.[1]

Joe Tom Meador was born in 1916 in Arkadelphia, Arkansas, and a year later moved with his family to Whitewright, Texas, where his father established a hardware and farm equipment store. Meador's mother had a deep interest in the arts and as a result of this passion, Meador received a Bachelor of Arts degree from North Texas State University. Later, he traveled to Biarritz, France, to study art. After he returned, Meador taught art in the local high school until he was inducted into the army on December 9, 1941, just two days after the surprise Japanese attack at Pearl Harbor.

Meador was commissioned a second lieutenant on August 28, 1942, and assigned to the 87th Armored Field Artillery. He arrived in England on January 8, 1944, and entered France via Normandy on June 9, 1944, three days after D-Day. As a forward observer directing artillery fire, he fought across Europe and participated in campaigns in Normandy, northern France, the Rhineland, Ardennes-Alsace, and in other places in central Europe. While advancing through these campaigns, he acquired altar pieces, paintings cut from their frames with a hunting knife, and numerous other rare treasures.

As the American army slogged into Germany, the Quedlinburg Church concealed its small treasure of aged ivory, precious stones, images of saints and kings, and crystal birds and fish, in a nearby tunnel of an unused mine. These valuable objects were symbols of the royal power of northern Europe, and were linked with the Byzantine and Roman empires through small bits of fabric and blood and bones inside reliquaries (a receptacle, such as a coffer or shrine, for keeping or displaying relics), several of which were believed to enshrine Christ's holy blood. On April 19, 1945, the United States army captured Quedlinburg and the mine containing the treasure was found and guarded by the 87th Armored Field Artillery.

Shortly after the mine was placed under army protection an official of the church, with military approval, went inside and inspected the religious artifacts. To his immense relief, it had not been disturbed. A few days passed before the church official inspected the treasure again. This time, however, two valuable bibles and the Reliquary of Henry I were missing. The missing reliquary was a 9th century wooden chest decorated with silver, ivory, gold, and precious stones. Several generations of creativity and craftsmanship from Frankish and German workshops had created this historic chest. The gospel scenes appearing on the chest are examples of some of the finest elephant ivory carvings in existence. The side panels on the chest portray the Apostles, and are carved from walrus ivory. Among many other ivory scenes, the reliquary shows Christ's mission to the Apostles, and the Three Marys at the tomb of Christ. Church officials reported the theft of this and other items to the U.S. Army commander on June 6, 1945. Over the next several days, more valuables disappeared from the mine.

The Reliquary of Henry I, a priceless 9th century chest.

Although we do not know exactly how these valuables fell into Meador's hands, we do know that he mailed them home to his mother in Texas. This treasure is valued today at more than $220 million. In addition to the Reliquary of Henry I, the Quedlinburg Church Treasure consisted of:

– The Evangelistic Samuels, a 10th century Saxon religious manuscript of the Four Gospels. Its gold covers are inlaid with precious jewels. This Samuel Gospel is one of the earliest Latin manuscripts and was named after the scribe who wrote it;

– The Evangelair Bible. This 1515 masterpiece has a one-piece cover of silver decorated with 13 precious stones. Inside are numerous medieval hand-drawn scenes;

– Old relics and an embroidered case;

– A reliquary in form of a plate, silvers (silvers???) and partly gilded. In the middle is an engraved image of Mary and Child, dating from about 1250;

– A spectacular 10th century rock crystal flask, its sides formed like birds of Byzantine origin, from Fatimid, Egypt;

The Evangelistic Samuels, a 10th century Saxon religious manuscript of the Four Gospels. Its gold covers are inlaid with precious jewels. This is one of the earliest Latin manuscripts and was named after the scribe who wrote it.

– The Comb of Henry I: An 8th century Egyptian elephant ivory comb with embedded gold, silver, and imitation pearls;

– Four small reliquaries originally designed to display enclosed relics;

– A reliquary in the form of a fish purported to contain hair from the Virgin Mary. This lovely artifact was given to the church by Emperor Otto II (955 - 983).

– A 10th century rock crystal relic shaped like a cone or triangle, with Latin inscription on both sides;

– Two turret shaped monstrance reliquaries made from rock crystal, gilt silver, garnets, and blue and green glass;

– A 15th century reliquary in form of a heart, inscribed *Agnus dei misere mei* (Lamb of God, have mercy on me.) The heart is a container for melted Easter wax, and was blessed by the Pope at the Lateran Basilica;

– A reliquary in the form of a plate with intarsia;

– A painted box containing sealed documents concerning the relics;

– old coins from a glass case;

– a pair of gold and silver crucifixes;

– several old embroideries;

– A memorial coin of Emperor Wilhelm II.[2]

After the cessation of hostilities in Europe, Lieutenant Meador returned to the art department of Biarritz University in France as a drawing instructor. There, he taught a variety of college-level courses to American soldiers as part of their continuing education in post-war Europe. The army requisitioned the Villa Banuelos, a property belonging to the Marquise of Saint Carlos, for use as an art school in August 1945. One room on the ground floor of the main building was reserved for the personal effects of the Marquise. This room of rugs, trunks, rare furniture, and bric-a-brac, was kept locked, with the key in the possession of the housekeeper, Elise Barbier.

The Evangelair Bible (1515). Its cover is one piece of silver decorated with 13 precious stones. This magnificent bible was made during the early days of print, and contains many medieval hand-drawn scenes.

This fish-shaped reliquary supposedly contained hair from the Virgin Mary.

On Saturday, October 6, 1945, Barbier opened the door of the personal effects room but forgot to remove the key from the lock. Some hours passed before she remembered the key. When she returned to fetch it, she discovered to her horror that it was missing and the door was open. She entered and found Lieutenant Meador standing in the center of the room. When she asked him for the missing key, he denied knowing its whereabouts. Later that day, however, Meador brazenly returned and put the key back in the door—in the presence of Barbier.

The next Monday, Barbier noticed that several pieces of silverware and china were missing from the room, along with a bone cigarette holder. The upset housekeeper reported the theft to Gerard Tourres, a French Policeman. The following day at 1:30 p.m., Tourres, along with Sergeant Gordon D. Howard of the U.S. Military Police, drove in Howard's jeep to the villa. There, Barbier identified Meador as the person who had stolen the key to the room from which the silverware, chinaware, and cigarette holder were missing. Howard asked Meador if the accusation was true, and whether Barbier had discovered him in the room. Meador adamantly denied both accusations.

Left with little choice, Howard informed Meador that his own room would have to be searched. Thus pressured, Meador admitted taking the items. He left and returned with a key to an upstairs cupboard from which the china was recovered. The silverware was found in Meador's room. According to Meador, "It [taking the items] was worth a chance."

Instead of riches, however, Meador's actions offered him the chance of jail. He was placed under house arrest and charged with stealing four dozen pieces of silverware and two dozen pieces of gold-decorated china. During his courts-martial an associate made the rather remarkable claim, given the circumstances, that the accused had a "very high degree of truth and honesty, and I would be willing to trust him with anything I had." This character testimony notwithstanding, Meador was found guilty after a one-day trial, severely reprimanded, and fined $600. "In view of the serious nature of your offense," admonished the judge, "the sentence imposed upon you by the court was thoroughly inadequate."[3]

After Lieutenant Joe Meador's honorable discharge from the army in 1946, he returned to East Texas and taught art at a school in New London. When his father became ill, Meador moved back to his family home in Whitewright and joined his brother Jack in running Meador, Inc., the hardware and farm equipment business founded by their father.

Friends and neighbors recalled that the war years had changed Meador from an outgoing and friendly young man to a secretive, mysterious recluse. As a hobby, he built three greenhouses and began raising orchids. Within a few years he had cultivated 6,200 orchids representing 129 varieties. Occasionally, Meador displayed old manuscripts at the family store with the explanation that he had acquired them in Europe at the end of the war. Visitors to his home came away impressed with his collection of antiques, beautiful rugs, and fine paintings. Had Joe Meador looted more than just the Quedlinburg Church Treasure and Marquise of Saint Carlos's silverware and China?

Unbeknownst to his neighbors and few friends, the reclusive Meador was living two lives. During the week he ran a hardware store; on the weekends, however, he traveled to Dallas and delved deeply into the night life there. At various bars he would launch into conversations about art. If someone demonstrated an interest in the topic, Meador invited them to a luxurious apartment he kept there, decorated with the Quedlinburg Church Treasure and other valuables stolen during the war. Meador never attempted to sell any of these artifacts, and after his death from cancer on February 1, 1980, the collection was discovered intact except for some valuables that might well have been stolen from the apartment by his male lovers.[4]

Meador left his estate to his brother, Jack, and his sister, Jean Meador Cook. His will whispered not a word about the Quedlinburg Treasure. In 1983, Mrs. Cook's husband, Dr. Don H. Cook, a dentist, asked John Carroll Collins, a Dallas-based estate appraiser, to examine a pair of old manuscripts. When he arrived at a lawyer's office, he found two women holding a large cardboard box. The women emptied the box by tossing one manuscript on top of the other, as if they were handling a pair of phone books. Collins, an expert in his field, immediately recognized one of them as part of the missing Quedlinburg collection. Barely able to contain his anger at the way the priceless books were being handled, Collins informed those in attendance that the manuscripts had been stolen and could not be legitimately sold.

Ultimately, the Evangelistic Samuels, the 10th century bejeweled religious manuscript, went on the art market in 1988 with an asking price of $9,000,000. John S. Torigian, a Dallas lawyer representing Jack Meador, offered the book to several major dealers, including the J. Paul Getty Museum. The manuscript was eventually sold to a West German foundation for a "finder's fee" of $3,000,000. The matter was handled through Switzerland, where privacy laws protect the identification of parties and other aspects of these types of transactions. Part of the deal was that the American owner's name would never be revealed. The manuscript's purchaser was Heribert Tenschert, a Bavarian art dealer who, in turn, sold it to a West German foundation in April 1990.

At that time, Klaus Goldmann, curator of the Museum for Ancient Arts in Berlin, notified Bill Honan of the *New York Times* that the Evangelistic Samuels manuscript from the Quedlinburg Church Treasure had surfaced. Honan contacted a number of rare book dealers for more information. Finally, a New York dealer admitted that he had seen a photograph of the book, which had been sent to him by a banker in Texas. Honan passed along the name of the dealer to Willi Korte, a German freelance expert in stolen art, who went to the dealer's shop and inquired about the photograph. The dealer refused to tell Korte where the photograph came from. However, he took out a map of Texas, placed a pencil on Whitewright, and left the room.

Korte left New York and returned to his home in Silver Springs, Maryland. A short time later he flew to Dallas, rented a car, and drove to Whitewright. On May 7, 1990, he stepped into the office of the president of First National Bank—the only bank in Whitewright. Korte introduced himself to the bank president and added, "I'm here because of the Quedlinburg Treasures." Unbeknownst to Korte, the valuables were only a few yards away in the bank vault. The president, however, was uncooperative and would not provide him with any information. Korte left empty-handed. His seven-word introduction, however, had stirred up a hornet's nest. The following day the bank called Korte and informed him that the institution's security policies required that it engage legal counsel.

Honan and Korte stayed on the trail. Honan checked with appraisers in the Dallas area and came up with the names Meador and Cook, and connections with a dead brother who had served in World War II. Because there were numerous Meadors and Cooks in eastern Texas, Honan began visiting local libraries and reviewing scrapbooks for clues that might assist him. In the library in the small town of Sherman, Texas, the indefatigable reporter hit pay dirt. The library's scrapbook about the local area had an article about a Joe Meador with a reference to his sister Jane Cook, and surviving brother Jack. Honan knew immediately he was close to solving the mystery of the stolen the Quedlinburg Treasure.

On behalf of the 450-member Quedlinburg Church, Korte hired the Washington-Dallas law firm of Andrew & Kurth and filed a lawsuit against Meador, Cook, and the First National Bank for the return of the valuables. Shortly thereafter, the treasure was moved from the bank vault to the Dallas Museum of Art for safekeeping. After considerable legal negotiations, in 1992 Jack and his sister turned over the treasure to German officials in an out-of-court settlement that earned them $2.75 million. On May 1, 1992, after two years of legal wrangling, the jewel-encrusted religious relics were returned to Quedlinburg, home of their royal past.[5]

On March 7, 1992, before the Quedlinburg Treasure was returned to Germany, the items went on display at the Dallas Museum of Art. To the amazement of several individuals who knew the unique history of the priceless artifacts, the display was utterly silent about the theft of the treasure and its legal history that now allowed it to be displayed.

Author Kenneth Alford (far left), and his son, Roger. The Alfords were among the first to visit the Dallas Museum of Art, and were shocked to discover that officials made no mention whatsoever of the fact that the treasure had been stolen, and was there as part of an out-of-court settlement. "I turned over a copy of my file, regarding the looting of the Quedlinburg Treasure, to museum officials, who reluctantly accepted it, with no acknowledgment or thank-you," explained the author. To this day, he explains, "most of the thousands of people who saw the exhibit have no real idea of its true history, which is really a shame."

Although the more valuable pieces of the Quedlinburg Church Treasure were recovered, the 10th century rock crystal relic and of gold and silver crucifixes from the 12th century are still missing. The History Channel recently aired an excellent program on the Quedlinburg Church Treasures and displayed pictures of the still-missing relics. Perhaps the dissemination of this information, together with the publication of this book, will help locate and restore these priceless items to their rightful owners.

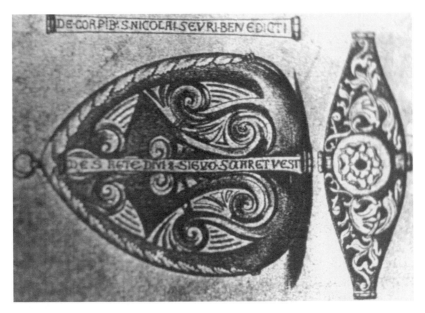

Still missing: A 10th century rock crystal relic (above) shaped like a cone or triangle with a Latin inscription on both sides. It has also been described as shaped like a bishop's hat. (Below) Two gold-and-silver crucifixes from the 12th century.

Chapter Nineteen

Adolf Eichmann's Treasure Map

Adolf Eichmann is known to history as the architect of the Final Solution—a simple euphemism for the mass murder of European Jews. His substantial logistical abilities, executed with cold-blooded efficiency, sent millions of men, women, and children to their deaths. His position within the Nazi hierarchy also offered him the opportunity to loot gold, currency, and other valuables on a vast scale.

Eichmann, born in 1906, was an SS officer and the head of the Jewish Evacuation Department of the Gestapo. He received his orders about the fate of the Jews from Heinrich Himmler in 1941 following the German invasion of Russia. Eichmann took great pleasure in executing Himmler's directive, which he carried out with brutal efficiency. With the war turning against the Germans, Eichmann left Prague, Czechoslovakia, and arrived in Alt Aussee in April 1945. He established various quarters at the Hotel Villa Kerry, the Park Hotel, and Hotel Penson Eibl. During his retreat from the advancing Russian army, Eichmann collected numerous chests of gold and foreign currency from Hungarian and Yugoslavian museums and churches. The treasures were collected and funneled into Vienna, and as the Germans withdrew from there, the valuables were dispatched to the Monastery at Kremsmünster. On May 3, 1945, the treasures were loaded onto a truck and an SS

SS officer Adolf Eichmann, the architect of the Final Solution, the mass murder of European Jews.

Officer, Rudolph Doskoczil, was given instructions to deliver the contents of the truck to Alt Aussee.

The following day, the fourth of May, an assembly of SS men gathered in front of the Park Hotel. The soldiers were busy selecting snow skis and other mountaineering equipment for the task of defending a mountain post at nearby Blaa-Alm (an alm is an Alpine pasture) against the approaching U.S. Army. Their commander was Adolf Eichmann.

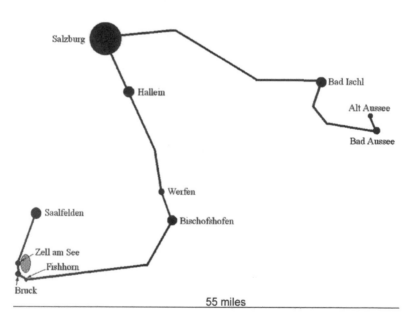

This map shows the various locations of Eichmann's frenzied schedule in Austria during the final days of World War II, during which time he managed to hide millions in gold, currency, and other loot.

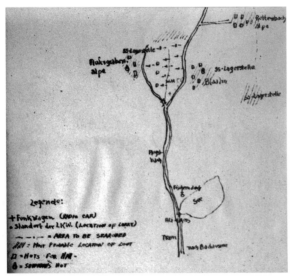

This remarkable map, prepared for U.S. Counter Intelligence by a German or Austrian informant in 1945 and published here for the first time, shows the Dead Mountain in Upper Austria and the purported location of Eichmann's treasure, as indicated by slash marks. The "+" in the fork of the dirt road near the top of the map is where Eichmann's burned radio car was found. The small boxes are shepherd huts. This map was discovered by the author in an unnumbered box in Record Group 38, National Archives, Washington, D.C.

The trip covered about five miles down a narrow dirt road. At Blaa-Alm, the two trucks and a radio car were parked about 150 yards from a small inn, and were guarded by SS troops with machine guns. The downstairs taproom was jammed full of SS men with weapons and rucksacks. Several administrative office girls were with the group. The "defenders" were drinking cognac and many were so drunk as to be completely helpless. As the American army advanced toward them Eichmann and his staff attempted to flee. An avalanche, however, skidded down the mountainside covered the road, blocking their route. Eichmann, it appeared, was trapped.

On May 8, the U.S. Army captured Alt Aussee and the deserted mountain defense post at Blaa-Alm. Two empty trucks were also recovered. Eichmann's staff had burned the radio car. The SS troops, mass murderer Adolf Eichmann, and the gold had disappeared. The SS

Treasure fever spread through the local population when several kilos of gold were discovered in one of the hay huts shown above at Blaa-Alm in 1982.

carried away some of the loot in rucksacks, but as it turned out, a large quantity of valuables was hidden or buried close to Blaa-Alm.[1]

Immediately after the arrival of the American troops in Alt Aussee, a salt miner and farmer, Johann Pucher, reported that he had unearthed three chests near the Villa Kerry Hotel. They were opened without too much difficulty with an acetylene torch, and found to contain 154 pounds of gold, 92,000 Swiss francs, $22,000 U.S. dollars, and 25,000 Dutch guldens. The treasure was delivered to Captain L. A. Degner, U.S. military government, 80th Infantry Division.

Three U.S. army privates guarding German prisoners at Alt Aussee stumbled across a bag lying along the side of the road. Much to their surprise, the bag was full of coins—703 gold U.S. $20 gold pieces. How the bad ended up next to the dirt road is unknown, but the gold was almost certainly part of Eichmann's cache.

Before long it became obvious that during the closing days of World War II, Adolf Eichmann buried some five tons of gold and other loot, much of it near the small village of Alt Aussee. U.S. Forces, however, never recovered the bulk of the gold at Blaa-Alm. Some of the precious

Published for the first time, this map was prepared by U.S. Counter Intelligence for a German or Austrian informant in 1945. Many believe gold and other valuables were dumped in Zell am See lake during the closing days of WWII. The author found this map in an unnumbered box in the National Archives in Washington, D.C.

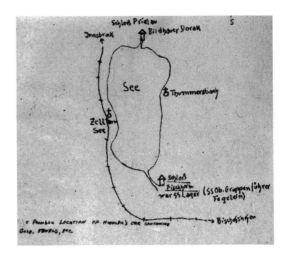

metal has been found in the area over the years, but the lion's share remains hidden.

While most of Eichmann's gold disappeared for good, Eichmann did not. The SS officer, one of the most sought-after criminals in history, slipped out of Europe with a Vatican passport under the alias "Ricardo Klement." For more than fifteen years he lived a quiet, if rather nerve-wracking, existence in South America. In 1961, Eichmann's luck ran out. Israeli agents, who had been hunting him since 1945, slipped into Argentina, seized him, and smuggled him out of the country and back to Israel. After a lengthy and emotional trial, during which Eichmann never showed an ounce of regret, he was found guilty of war crimes and hanged.

Another area that has generated concentrated searches for Nazi loot near the scene Eichmann's final frenzied days of the war is the Austrian village of Zell am See. It was here, according to notes found in U.S. Army Counter Intelligence Corps files, that Heinrich Himmler's Mercedes was purportedly filled with gold, jewels, and other valuables and dumped into the southern portion of the lake. The north side of the lake by Prielau castle is also believed to be an area containing a large quantity of valuables. The lake belongs to the town of Zell, and no one is allowed to probe into its depths. About five years ago, however, a bronze bust of Hitler was found in its waters. What else lies beneath its placid surface?

Chapter Twenty

The Mystery of the Missing Amber Room

The fate of the magnificent Amber Room is the one of the greatest lingering remaining mysteries of World War II. A detailed history of the remarkable Amber Room is necessary to fully appreciate its former splendor and the impact of its loss.

The best information attributes its 1699 design to Andreas Schluter, the architect of the Prussian royal court. When the Great Royal Palace in Berlin, commissioned by Friederich I (1657- 1713), was being reconstructed, Schluter came up with the idea of employing amber to finish one of the palace rooms. The thought was considered revolutionary, since the material had never been used for interior decoration anywhere in the world. Schulter's recommendation was made easier by the fact that the king's massive amber collection was stored nearby.

The basis for the adornment was a triumvirate of 17th century richly decorated amber frames with windows. In 1701, the architect, who was not accustomed to working with amber, invited Gottfried Wolfram, an amber expert working for Danish King Friedrich IV, to assist him with the plans. The project was never finished. For reasons that are not entirely clear, Schluter left Berlin after being dismissed. A Swedish architect named Eosander von Goethe, hired to replace him, did not get along with Wolfram, who soon followed in Schluter's footsteps. A frustrated

Friederich I decided to finish the plans at Charlottenburg castle, and the amber fragments were hauled there. Six years after the project began, an agreement was reached to continue and finish the work when two amber masters from Danzig arrived at the castle. Gottfried Turau and Ernest Schacht labored for almost six years. Amber was polished and cut into interlocking jigsaw pieces to form mosaics of exquisite floral scroll work, busts, and other symbols. Unfortunately, the death of Friederich I in February, 1713, ground the project to a halt. The new Prussian king, Friederich Wilhelm I, had not interest in an amber room. The blueprints for the Amber Room were shipped to Berlin and soon forgotten.

Eventually, news of the remarkable amber plans leaked into Russia, and Emperor Peter I (Peter the Great) decided to obtain them and the amber for himself. His opportunity arrived in 1716 when he met with Friedrich Wilhelm I outside Berlin. Anxious to cultivate the Russian's friendship, the Prussian king offered the plans and amber as a gift. Count Alexei Golovin, the emperor's diplomat in Berlin, arranged the transfer of eighteen boxes of amber to Koenigsburg, and thence to Memel. After a lengthy journey by wagon, the amber arrived in St. Petersburg, where it was stored in the Peter I's Summer Palace. Other matters occupied his attention, and when Peter the Great died in 1725, the amber was still languishing in storage.

Empress Elizabeth took over the throne in 1741 and, learning of the amber pieces, decided to use them to complete one of the rooms in her official residence. The difficult task was assigned to her architect, Bartolomeo Francesco Rastrelli. As the project unfolded, Rastrelli sought assistance in 1743 from Italian Alexander Martelli. Imitation amber panels and mirrors were utilized to disguise the fact that there was not enough amber to completely adorn the large room in the Winter Palace.

When the Amber Room was finally completed in 1746, it witnessed grand official receptions and gatherings. Nine years later, in July of 1755, Empress Elizabeth directed Rastrelli to create an Amber Room in the Great Palace. The existing Amber Room was carefully taken apart and packed for its journey from the St. Petersburg Winter Palace to Tzarskoje Selo. The room chosen to house the amber was too large for the existing amber display. Using the same techniques as before (as well as fake paintings of amber) the room was finished, complete with carved and

The magnificent Amber Room, much as it looked when it was finished in 1770. This image was taken in the 1930s.

gilded sculptures. So delicate was the display that a special amber steward, Friedrich Roggenbuch, was designated oversee its upkeep.

Empress Catherine II (Catherine the Great), however, was not content with an Amber Room that was only partially made of amber. In 1763, she ordered Roggenbuch to finish the room with the real material. The planning and work took seven years and 450 kilograms of amber. The legendary Amber Room was finally complete. Russia's climate, however, was hard on the fragile display, and during the next century the room was restored three times (1833, 1865, and 1893-1897). Minor repairs were also effected during the 1920s and 1930s. A complete restoration of the room of amber was scheduled for 1941. Other events, however, interrupted these plans.

Although Josef Stalin and his generals expected Russia would have to eventually fight a war with Germany, when it came they were utterly unprepared for the rapacious conflict Hitler waged. On June 22, 1941, 153 divisions in three army groups, supported by another three tactical air forces, unleashed Hitler's Operation Barbarossa. The lightening speed and staggering power of the overwhelming attack—Hitler's invasion

(Above) Catherine the Great's Palace. (Below) A panel from the missing Amber Room.

comprised the largest invading force in European history—swept through western Russia and St. Petersburg in September 1941.

The Wehrmacht took over Catherine the Great's Palace as a headquarters building, and in short order removed the Amber Room panels. Like a huge jigsaw puzzle, these priceless pieces were glued to

large panels of wood and mounted onto the walls. One large panel was a relief of the two-headed eagle of the Russian Czars. The pillaging Germans packed the panels of the Amber Room into twenty-five large crates and shipped them to the Baltic seaport of Königsberg. Renamed Kaliningrad after the war, Königsberg hosted and prominently displayed stolen art during the period of German occupation.

Gauleiter Erich Koch, a Königsberg-born Prussian whose commands during his Russian tenure sent thousands to their deaths, was in charge of the Amber Room in the last few weeks before the Red Army surrounded and destroyed the German defenses. If the Russian authorities were looking forward to retrieving the precious panels, they were sorely disappointed. On the eve of the Red Army victory, the extraordinary gift from King Frederich Wilhelm I to Czar Peter the Great vanished.

After the war, Koch was captured near Hamburg in 1949 while living under the name of "Major Berger." Koch was sent to a Polish prison in 1950, and after nine long years, sentenced to death for his war crimes. Koch allegedly suffered from poor health, which effectively transformed his death sentence into life in prison. He was aggressively interrogated about the Amber Room, as well as other thefts of significant magnitude. If he knew of its fate, however, he never revealed its whereabouts. Koch died in custody in 1986.

The Amber Room's mysterious disappearance has generated a host of competing theories. Speculation has the treasure hidden secreted underground near a Roman Catholic church, buried in a cemetery, or hidden in the cellar of a local beer brewery. Over the years various groups in Königsberg have searched for the treasure in these locations—and hundreds more. The Secret Russian police (KGB) and Secret East German police (Stassi) spent years amassing large files and probing for the missing Amber Room, all in vain.

One story holds that the room of amber, packed in crates, was shipped from Königsberg to Danzig, where it was loaded onto the Hamburg-bound *Wilhelm Gustloff*. The ship sailed on January 30, 1945, with more than 9,000 passengers. Unfortunately, the liner was torpedoed by S-13, a Russian submarine. Some 8,000 souls went down with the ship. The Amber Room, according to this theory, went to the bottom of the Baltic Sea with the *Wilhelm Gustloff*, where it remains to this day. This little-known sinking is the largest maritime disaster in history—five times as many people died on the *Wilhelm Gustloff* than on the ill-fated *Titanic*. Yet, few know of her tragic fate.

Other versions of the treasure's whereabouts involve the American army. According to one popular theory, the missing amber panels were shipped by trucks from Königsberg to Frankfurt am Oder, transferred to a train, and then taken to Buch, an underground rail station near Berlin. From there the Amber Room was shipped, the story goes, to Weimar and stored in the Thuringia State Museum. On April 9, 1945, two International Red Cross trucks were stolen and the Amber Room was loaded onto the trucks and sent north to Grasleben or Nordhausen. The U.S. 35th Infantry Division captured Grasleben on April 12, 1945. The Grasleben Mine contained the official records of 89 of Germany largest cities, 12,000 tape recordings belonging to the German radio network, complete libraries from leading universities, and major works of art from the museums of Berlin.

On May 4, 1945, Lieutenant Lamont Moore, a Monuments and Fine Arts Officer, went to Grasleben and searched the large tunnels. On May 10, Moore located and removed the Treasure of the Cathedral of Posen, taken by the Germans from Poland, which contained four cases labeled "Posen Domkirchen," two cases labeled "Lissa Collections," and several hundred cases said to contain gold and silver monstrance and shrines. T Force, Twelfth Army Group, moved into Grasleben two days later, and its 120-man detail took charge of the mine and its contents.

On June 18, 1945, a mysterious fire erupted in the mine chamber containing the film archives; the mine remained inaccessible until June 26. Almost two months later on August 17, the area came under British control. The British established that ten percent of the contents of the mine had been removed by the Americans and more than half of the remaining 6,800 cases had been torn open and rifled. Between the time the American forces arrived and the time the mine was taken over by the British, fifteen percent of the finest art from the Berlin museums had disappeared. Neither the records nor the art has ever been recovered.

Both American and British authorities claim that these invaluable items were burned in the fire. Was the Amber Room at Grasleben, and stolen by the American or British, or was it perhaps destroyed during the fire? This and many other questions regarding the missing artwork

The Treasure of the Cathedral of Posen, on display for a handful of American soldiers at the Foreign Exchange Depository, Frankfurt, Germany. Lieutenant Lamont Moore, working for the U.S. Army, removed the treasure from the Grasleben Mine.

remain unanswered. The activity of the American Army at Grasleben is still shrouded in almost complete secrecy.[1]

Indeed, even Lieutenant Moore refused to publicly discuss his role in the Gasleben Mine. When questioned during a telephone interview by the author about the Amber Room and other valuables at Grasleben, Moore claimed he had never entered the Gasleben facility. Confronted with the knowledge that the author was in possession of photographs clearly showing Moore's participation in the recovery of items from the Grasleben Mine, Moore said, "My lips are sealed to the grave," and quickly hung up.[2]

In April 1945, the Americans arrived at Nordhausen, the other suspected site of the Amber Room. From the Mittelbau Dora, an underground facility at Nordhausen, one of the grand prizes of World War II was discovered: the advanced technical material developed by German scientists. The Mittelbau Dora complex, built by slave labor, was made up of 46 chambers over 200 yards wide and two connecting tunnels 1.5 miles long. A railroad track and overhead crane trolley ran down both tunnels. In addition to hauling materials, the overhead crane was used to hang slave laborers for low production. Of the 60,000 prisoners who participated in the construction of Mittelbau Dora, one-third died from exhaustion and starvation in the hell-hole often simply known as called "Dora."[3]

After the horrifying task of burying 3,000 rotting corpses of slave labor camp victims at Nordhausen, the U.S. Army removed 100 V-2 rockets, 1,420 tons of scientific documents, and 46 tons of microfilm from Mittelbau Dora. These materials, together with 350 German specialists, were shipped to White Sands, New Mexico, and Wright-Patterson Air Base. Some remaining V-2 rockets and the equipment to manufacture them were left for the occupying Russians. In their naivete, the Americans did not foresee that the Russians would modify this equipment and use it a dozen years later to launch Sputnik, the world's first artificial satellite, thereby triggering the space race. Some Amber Room buffs believe that in their haste to remove the high-tech weapons before the Russian moved in, the Americans overlooked the treasure that once adorned Catherine the Great's palace.

Paul Enke and Georg Stein, two longtime researchers of the Amber Room mystery, concluded independently that the treasure was actually discovered by U.S. forces in an underground depot and shipped to America. Today, their conclusions seem doubtful. If the U.S. Army had seized a treasure as grand and famous as the Amber Room from either Grasleben or Nordhausen, it would have been next to impossible to keep secret for over half a century.[4]

In 1992, Russian President Boris Yeltsin claimed that Russian KGB reports conclude that the Amber Room was still buried in the Thuringia Provence (i.e., Mittelbau Dora). His statement set off a round of frenzied treasure fever in the Thuringia. Wolfgang Schneider, another dedicated Amber Room researcher, concluded later that year that the Amber had indeed been hidden in the underground complex behind tons of dynamited rock:

Global Explorations, searching the Freckleben castle
grounds for the lost Amber Room.

As the 80th Infantry Division advanced towards Weimar, Dr. Walter
Scheidig, Director of the Thuringia State Museum, asserted that the Amber
Room was loaded upon two International Red Cross trucks.

The trucks were under command of General Hans Kammler, the director
of V1, V2 research and architect of the notorious Dora Concentration
Camp. Using ten-of-thousands of these prisoners, Kammler had
constructed a state-of-the-art underground armament facility. The facility
was in Nordhausen and was given the name Mittelbau Dora. Kammler had
the trucks drive the Amber Room to the Mittelbau Dora facility, store the
amber in one of the chambers, and then dynamite it shut.[5]

Drilling on the Freckleben castle grounds for the lost Amber Room.

Schneider's detailed claims convinced a Florida-based operation named Global Explorations to launch an investigation of the Mittelbau Dora tunnels. This proved to be far more difficult than anticipated. After the Russians removed the V2s and equipment from Mittelbau Dora, they dynamited the complex and completely collapsed the granite mountain housing the underground factory. It was easier to tunnel down the side and then cross over into the former production facility than remove the tons of stone from Mittelbau Dora. A large sum of money was spent digging the new side tunnel and entering the various chambers. Nothing of value was found.

Global Explorations, however, soon turned its attention elsewhere. New information on the Amber Room seeped in from a former East German ambassador to the Dominican Republic, who claimed his information had been culled from the vast Stassi (East German) files. He offered to sell the location of the Amber Room. The document, signed by Heinrich Himmler and Adolf Hitler, reflected that the treasure was moved from Königsberg to Weimar and sent on the way to Nordhausen in two International Red Cross trucks. Cut off by the advancing 3rd Armored Division, the trucks turned and headed east on secondary roads. The American First Army quickly advanced beyond the trucks. Finding themselves surrounded in the small village of Freckleben, General Hans Kammler's party took the Amber Room to Freckleben castle, which overlooked the village. The crates of amber, continued the information from the Stassi files, were placed in a tunnel located under the castle and the entrance was dynamited shut. It was only a matter of digging the dirt from the entrance and removing the crates containing the Amber Room.

An arrangement was made for Global Explorations to acquire the documents from former Stassi files. Large sums of money were spent, grids were charted, holes were drilled, and dirt was removed from the Freckleben castle grounds.

The Amber Room, however, was nowhere to be found.

– Chapter Twenty-One –

The Library of Congress Mission

I mmediately following World War II, the Library of Congress recognized the urgent need to acquire German material published between 1939 and 1945. Missions were dispatched to the main German cities to make arrangements to obtain wartime publications. By the fall of 1945, the Library of Congress had established mission offices in Berlin, Wiesbaden, Frankfurt, and Munich. There were eventually twenty-six American librarians and document specialists employed in Germany and Austria by the Library of Congress.

According to Reuben Peiss, Deputy Library Congress Mission, the purpose was "to get what is to be got, to distribute this to American libraries, and then go after the gaps which show up in our holdings when the inventory has been made."[1] In other words, the Library of Congress was to grab whatever it could get its hands on and ship it to the United States. The mission was very effective. A grand total of 819,022 non-Nazi books and more than 1,000,000 periodicals were shipped to the Library of Congress in Washington, D.C. Among the most notable items obtained from Germany were an 1815 translation of the German epic *Das Lied der Nibelungen*, by Johann Gustav Büschung, and a first edition (1776) of Goethe's *Stella: ein Schauspiel für iebende in fünf Akten*.

In addition to the non-Nazi-related books, the Library of Congress acquired 141 "tendentious" collections of books, pamphlets, bound sets

Members of the Library of Congress Mission in Germany. Third from left (with glasses) is Reuben Peiss, Deputy Library of Congress Mission.

of periodicals, newspapers, photographs, maps, and other miscellaneous items. These confiscated items were shipped in 7,598 containers, which contained an estimated 1,500,000 items.

But was the wholesale seizure of these items legally justifiable or even morally correct? Reuben Peiss, Deputy Library of Congress Mission, thought so, although he acknowledged in a March 23, 1946, letter to Luther H. Evans, Director of the Library of Congress, that others disagreed with his assessment:

> The first thing to keep in mind is that eight or nine out of ever ten confiscated volumes that find their way into the Library of Congress will have been collected and shipped by Army document teams. . . . I will not maintain that in the vast sweep of the document teams some of the materials may not have been scooped up which ought to have remained untouched. . . Malpractice has undoubtedly occurred at times, as it will in any large operation, and we ought to keep our eyes open for chances to correct such malpractice, but I am convinced of the moral cleanliness of the operation as a whole. It is only fair to point out here that others do not share that convection. One day we are going to face accusations and we may find we have made unwise decisions on a few specific issues, but I think we shall continue to have a clear conscience.

The largest World War II collection acquired by the Library of Congress was the Friedrich Rehse Collection. Josef Maria Rehse was born on March 23, 1870, in Muenster, Germany. A photographer and lithographer by profession, he served as an apprentice in Brussels and finally settled in Munich in 1898. He was an enterprising young man, selling photographs and designing posters. He began collecting political posters, books, pamphlets, newspapers, periodicals, caricatures, and newspaper clippings. Eventually, his collection boasted ten of thousands of these items, which Rehse arranged chronologically in a catalog.

The collapse of the German economy after the loss of World War I, however, ushered in hard economic times for Rehse. In 1928, destitute and with no hope of acquiring additional funds, Rehse decided to sell his mammoth collection. He received several high bids, including an offer from the Hoover War Library. The Nazi Party stepped in at the last moment, purchased the Rehse documents, appointed their former owner Director of Collections, and provided him a life pension. The massive assortment of paper—one item of special interest is a manuscript war diary for the year 1916–1917 by Hans Baumann, whose journal contains numerous photographs with pencil drawings on postcards, and is bound in velvet with heavy silver ornaments—was moved into fifty rooms in the basement of the Kaiserhof of the Munich Residenz. Several large exhibitions were arranged for this collection over the ensuring years.

During World War II, however, Allied bombing runs forced Rehse to move a large portion of the collection to the basement of the Burgerbrau. The Nazi Party had used this building as a meeting place and for a variety of exhibitions. Hitler founded the Nazi Party at the Burgerbrau, where he attempted his famous beer hall putsch of November 9, 1923. After the capture of Munich, T Force visited the Burgerbrau cellar and inspected its condition. Although the upper floors had been heavily bombed, the ground floor and basement were largely undamaged.

In the fall of 1945, some 100 cases of the Rehse collection were removed from the Residenz and the Burgerbrau and stored in the Munich Collection Point. Afterwards the Rehse Collection was sent from Munich to the Library of Congress. During the shipping process, Don Travis, a representative from the Library of Congress, was on hand when Rehse visited the Munich Collection Point with Hans Beilback. Out of sight, Travis eavesdropped on their conversation as the 77-year-old Rehse complained about the loss of his life's work, his innocence, and the removal of the collection by the occupying powers. After listening for

The basement of the Burgerbrau Cellar, which contained several hundred thousand books, is being examined by Hans Beilhach, an employee with the Library of Congress. Masses of books were piled in corners arranged on shelves, and stored in big wooden boxes. The items included Vestments, Torahs, Talmuds, and Masonic items and art objects—in addition to papers, newspapers, and handwritten manuscripts. There were also many unopened crates marked "NSDAP Reichsleitung."

several minutes, Travis appeared and vanquished the old man with several statements regarding the Library of Congress's rights to confiscating Nazi Party material. "He is an earnest collector and had brought together an extremely unusual collection of ephemera," Travis later reported, "but in the development and arrangement of this stuff he also has shown himself an incorrigible dilettante." Travis concluded his letter by writing that he had finally convinced Rehse that "the matter is a closed affair and that all hope of recovery is gone."[2]

A few items from the Rehse Collection—which in total offered a broad insiders view of Germany between the two World Wars—were not recovered. These included a military uniform collection and a large assortment of pornographic materials. Since both uniforms and nude photographs would have been of some interest to souvenir hunters, perhaps that explains their eventual fate.

After lengthy negotiations, in the fall of 1982, the Manuscript Division of the Library of Congress agreed to return a few of the seized collections—including the Rehse collection—to the Bundesarchiv in Koblenz, Germany. The collection was microfilmed and the source items returned to their homeland. Today, however, many original documents and books housed in the Library of Congress are imprinted with the telltale markings of their origins, such as the Rehse stamp. The Library of Congress simply kept the best and returned the rest.

The Library of Congress, via the United States Army, also collected thousands of books that once comprised Adolf Hitler's personal library. These books were taken from the Berghof, Hitler's mountain retreat near Berchtesgaden, his residence in Munich, a salt mine in Alt Ausse, and a warehouse in Berchtesgaden that contained Hitler's books from the Reich Chancellery in Berlin.

These publications were officially turned over to the Library of Congress but remained at Freising, about 25 miles north of Munich, until 1952. The decision to maintain Hitler's former book collection in Freising for seven years could not have pleased anyone more than it pleased Hans Beilhach, a German civilian who worked for the Library of Congress. Books were his passion, and the Hitler Collection was his pride and joy. Beilhach kept them carefully inside locked cases and shelves, and dedicated a considerable amount of time studied them. The books were always displayed for visitors, and indeed when it was time to send

The Rehse collection stored in a corridor at the Munich Collection Point.

Some of the more interesting parts of the Rehse Collection still in the Library of Congress include the inflation currency (above, both photos), World War I posters, broadsides, handbills, pamphlets, field postcards with cartoons, POW correspondence, and extra editions of newspapers announcing victory in France and the Balkans.

them to Washington, explicit orders had to be passed to Beilhach to pack the books and send them to the Library of Congress.[3]

During the process of storing and shipping the books, Edgar Breitenbach, a Monuments Fine Art and Archives employee later employed by the Library of Congress, grabbed three of the Hitler books for his own collection. The titles stolen were Hitler's own *Mein Kampf*; Jacob Burckhardt's *Weltgeschichtliche*, and Johann Wolfgang Goethe's *Gedichte of Goethe*.

Adolf Hitler's ex-libris stamp.

Burckhardt's *Weltgeschichtliche Betrachtungen* was signed "Joe Burchhardt" on the title page. The inscription on the flyleaf to Hitler was written by Else Bruckmann, who penned that he was her "friend and Führer with greetings and celebration from Christmas, in old fidelity, Else Bruckmann, Munich, December 24, 1934. "The 80-year-old Else had been one of the first Nazi Party members in Munich.

The third book, by Goethe, was inscribed on the title page "Adolf Hitler, this picture book is from the book garden of Eva Chamberlain—for conversations in serious lonely hours." Eva was German composer Richard Wagner's daughter, and was married to British turncoat and prolific author Houston Stewart Chamberlain. The book contained four photographs and a presentation card from Siegfried and Winifred Wagner. Siegfried was Richard's son. After Siegfried's death in 1930, Winifred, born in England in 1897 and 25 years younger than her deceased husband, developed a close friendship with Hitler. To the end of her life Winifred Wagner remained an admirer of the Nazi leader. "To have met him" she explained in 1973, "is an experience I would not have missed."

In addition to numerous books inscribed to Hitler as birthday presents, his collection contains two titles pertaining to Houston Chamberlain. One, *Wrote Christi*, is inscribed to Hitler and has selections from the New Testament with an introduction and notes from Chamberlain. The other, *Life Work of H. S. Chamberlain in Outline*, is inscribed to Hitler by the publisher. To no one's surprise, several books on Richard Wagner (1813–1888) were discovered in Hitler's collection. The composer's music had an immense influence on Hitler, who was inspired in his youth by the powerful compositions and knew by heart the words of many of Wagner's operas. Ironically, both men were vegetarians, loners, and shared an intense dislike of Jews.

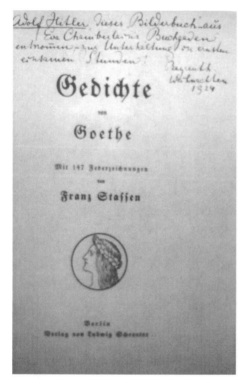

Johann Wolfgang Goethe's *Gedichte of Goethe*, from Hitler's personal library.

Today, the former private library of Adolf Hitler is housed in the Library of Congress's Rare Book Room. The collection is comprised of approximately 2,000 books and other miscellaneous materials. One of the major problems faced by Library of Congress employees was to deciding which books had actually been in the possession of the Führer. A standard was finally determined upon. Only those titles with Hitler's ex libris dedications to him, or accession numbers proceeded by the letters R. K. for Reichskanzlei (Reich Chancellery) inscribed in pencil on the fly leaf of the book were catalogued into the Library of Congress.

Decades later, the Library received three additional titles for the Hitler Collection. On October 4, 1991, Edgar Breitenbach's widow donated the three books he had snatched in 1945 from the collection while it was still housed in Munich.

Hitler's Collection also contains a large number of personal articles donated by a variety of authors, publishers, and gift-givers. The most common items were bookmarks and postcards advertising the book and/or publisher. The postcards usually represented order forms for additional books. Many of the titles housed letters folded inside addressing a range of topics from currency reform to work schedules. One of the more interesting inscriptions and personal letters are found in a book titled *Belcanto*, presented to Hitler by the author Hjalmar Arlberg. The inscription reads: "to the reverent Führer with a dedication to the

Arturo Toscanini." The dedication goes on to mention Hitler's former sweetheart, Winifred Wagner, who in the summer of 1931 entertained Toscanini with singing methods at her home in Bayreuth. A pair of letters, still in their original envelopes, were also inside *Belcanto*. Both were addressed to a "Fritz Arlberg" in Stockholm and Dresden. The book contained the author's business card and a newspaper clipping featuring an article on a new high school in Italy.

Surprisingly, a hundred or so of Hitler's books are of a serious religious nature. *Sermon on the Mount, Prayer and Christianity, Meditations, Worte Christi, Volk Blut and Gott and Jesus Christ, a Biography*, are just a few of these. *Kommet und vereinet euch im Volkerbund Gottes* offers the following inscription, which is representative of many found in Hitler's religious titles: "The very loved and deserving chancellor of the German Empire, Adolf Hitler, the true grapevine of the empire, God, the people of God, the Emmanuel of one for all and all for one."

The majority of the books found in the Adolf Hitler Collection, however, deal with or are related to the Nazi Party and it leaders, history, and ideological background. Conspicuously absent are German classics and works of fiction. Many were written and signed by some of Hitler's most fervent followers. Some of the more unusual books in Hitler's library are about vegetarian cuisine, meditation, and cost accounting. One book, *Metaphysische Problems*, contains the rather remarkable dedication: "To the admired sister of our Führer in his devotion. Christmas, 1935." What makes this otherwise mundane inscription uncommon is that few knew Hitler even had a sister, for he demanded she live under the last name "Wolff."

The Adolf Hitler Collection also holds books from other high-ranking Nazi collections, including titles that once belonged to Hermann Göring, Joseph Goebbels, Sepp Dietrich, Hans Frank, Heinrich Himmler, Alfred Rosenberg, Franz Xavier Schwartz, Julius Streicher, and Martin Bormann. Because of their value, these books—identified by their bookplates, dedications, or signatures, were catalogued as a supplement in the Hitler Library by the Library of Congress.

Heinrich Himmler's library was found intact in his Bavarian villa, Haus Schmeewinkel, which he had built for his 32-year-old mistress, Hedwig Potthast. "These documents will throw considerable light on

Himmler's private life and early activities," reported a T Force memorandum. "They will be indispensable should anyone ever want to write the real life story of Himmler. Himmler had the habit of inscribing his name and date of reading on the flyleaf of each book, thus providing considerable biographical documentation of his books." Unfortunately, Himmler's books were placed into the library's main collection of 115 million items.

Postscript

A staggering array of priceless artifacts stolen during World War II are still missing and waiting to be discovered. Thousands of treasure hunters from around the world have devoted decades of their lives searching for the missing jewels, art, gold, and other relics that vanished during the war—much of it during the final days of the conflict or immediately thereafter. Tantalizing finds spark continued interest and renewed hope.

Recently, a single marble mosaic panel from the Amber Room, valued at $2,500,000, surfaced in the attic of a long-deceased German veteran. Is the elusive Amber Room still in existence and waiting to be found? Or was it scattered to the winds and picked apart piecemeal by individuals? Perhaps the once magnificent golden Amber chamber of Catherine the Great is sealed beneath tons of rock in an abandoned salt mine, or simply disintegrating at the bottom of the sea in the wrecked hulk of the *Wilhelm Gustloff.*

And what became of the priceless box of Honor Rings? These rings were presented to ranking members of the SS by the head of that terrorist organization, Heinrich Himmler. The missing Honor Rings belonging to ranking SS dead, including Reinhard Heydrich, were collected and displayed in a "Ring of Honor" at the refurbished historic Wewelsburg Castle, in the district of Büren. It was there that Himmler held his SS services emulating the Ignatius Loyola spiritual exercises, ordaining SS members into senior positions. To Himmler, the Honor Rings were analogous to the honors bestowed on esteemed Jesuit Priests. The rings disappeared when the castle was captured by the US 3rd Armored Division. Many serious treasure hunters and researchers have spent years searching for the elusive container that once held the SS artifacts. Today, Reinhard Heydrich's ring alone would fetch upwards of $1,000,000. Is the legendary receptacle buried beneath the burned-out Wewelsburg castle?

And what of the hundreds of personal letters written between Adolf Hitler and Eva Braun? These letters are known to exist in the hands of a private collector in New Mexico. An esteemed publishing house has offered $5,000,000 just for *copies* of this private correspondence. Recently, the same collector attempted to sell the tunic worn by Hitler in July 1944 during the attempt on his life. In his possession also is the dress Eva Braun was wearing when she married Hitler in his Berlin Bunker hours before the couple took their own lives. What else does this collector have hidden away?

Perhaps Lucas Cranach's *The Venus* is hanging today in the corner of a dusty antique shop, its priceless worth unknown by those who cast their eyes upon her. Is Memling's *Madonna With Child* sealed behind a worthless oil canvas, adorning a plaster wall in a home tucked away in one of America's hundreds of suburbs? And where are the other thousands of paintings, coins, jewels, statues, religious vessels, and artifacts today?

The only thing we can be confident of is this: the search for lost World War II treasures will continue unabated for as long as they remain lost.

Appendix

Gold Germany took from Occupied Countries 1939 - 1945

	Troy Ounces	Pounds	Tons	1945 Dollars
Belgian	5,224,368	435,364	217.68	$182,852,880
Luxemburg	114,288	9,524	4.76	$4,000,080
Austria	2,531,028	210,919	105.46	$88,585,980
Vienna	142,596	11,883	5.94	$4,990,860
Holland	1,710,588	142,549	71.27	$59,870,580
Amsterdam	247,092	20,591	10.30	$8,648,220
Defense Fund				
Begium. France, Holland	1,425,408	118,784	59.39	$49,889,280
Italy	1,615,344	134,612	67.31	$56,537,040
Sudetenland	380,160	31,680	15.84	$13,305,600
Total	**13,390,872**	**1,115,906**	**557.95**	**$468,680,520**
Germany's Pre-war Gold Reserves	828,571	69,048	34.52	$29,000,000
Total World War II German Gold	**14,219,443**	**1,184,954**	**592.48**	**$497,680,520**

Gold Recovered at the End of World War II by the U.S. Army and Deposited in the Foreign Exchange Depository (FED), Frankfurt, Germany

Gold Recovered From				
1 Merkers	6,836,709	569,726	284.86	$239,284,815
2 Reichsbank Halle	25,682	2,140	1.07	$898,870
4 Reichsbank Plauen	25,296	2,108	1.05	$885,360
5 Reichsbank Nordhaus	22	2	0.00	$770
7 Reichsbank Eschwege	32,482	2,707	1.35	$1,136,870
10 Reichsbank Coburg	32,668	2,722	1.36	$1,143,380
15 Reichsbank Nuremburg	43,588	3,632	1.82	$1,525,580
21 Reichsbank Munich	175	15	0.01	$6,125
22 Friedrich	5,276	440	0.22	$184,660
26 Reichsbank Regensburg	11,930	994	0.50	$417,550
26 Haywagon	491	41	0.02	$17,185
27 Innsbruck	43,539	3,628	1.81	$1,523,865
27 Dorenwald	31,707	2,642	1.32	$1,109,745
27 Lindau	49,341	4,112	2.06	$1,726,935
27 Wallgau	290,584	24,215	12.11	$10,170,440
29 Reichsbank Zwicka	32,638	2,720	1.36	$1,142,330
31 Salzburg	333	28	0.01	$11,655
34 Reichsbank Kothen	894	75	0.04	$31,290
52 Garmisch	5,697	475	0.24	$199,395
52 Garmisch	23,021	1,918	0.96	$805,735
20 Hungarian Gold Reserves	919,292	76,608	38.30	$32,175,220
Gold Recovered by the U.S. Army	8,411,365	700,947	350.47	$294,397,775
Gold Returned to Hungary	919,292	76,608	38.30	$32,175,220
Total Gold in U.S. Army Custody	**7,492,073**	**624,339**	**312.17**	**$262,222,555**
Gold Shipped from FED to England	4,151,917	345,993	173.00	$145,317,095
Gold in Germany after Shipment	**3,340,156**	**278,346**	**139.17**	**$116,905,460**

Bank of England Gold Pot	Troy Ounces	Pounds	Tons	1945 Dollars
Gold Shipped from FED to England	4,151,917	345,993	173.00	$145,317,095
Austria March 1950	2,965	247	0.12	$103,775
Spain Feb 1949	3,267	272	0.14	$114,345
Romania Apr 1948	578,700	48,225	24.11	$20,254,500
Bank Int'l Settlement July 48	89,560	7,463	3.73	$3,134,600
Bank Int'l Settlement July 48	30,684	2,557	1.28	$1,073,940
Allied Gold in Bank of England	**4,857,093**	**404,758**	**202.38**	**$169,998,255**
U.S. Federal Reserve Gold Pot				
Acquired from Sweden Dec 1948	230,049	19,171	9.59	$8,051,715
Acquired from Switzerland Jun 47	1,659,121	138,260	69.13	$58,069,235
Total in N.Y. Federal Reserves	**1,889,170**	**157,431**	**78.72**	**$66,120,950**
Total In Gold Pot	**10,086,419**	**840,535**	**420.27**	**$353,024,665**
Return to Austria	1,276,932	106,411	53.21	$44,692,620
Return to France	3,440,193	286,683	143.34	$120,406,755
Return to Italy	284,628	23,719	11.86	$9,961,980
Return to Holland	2,139,235	178,270	89.13	$74,873,225
Return to Czechoslovakia	195,283	16,274	8.14	$6,834,905
Return to Yugoslavia	276,760	23,063	11.53	$9,686,600
Miscellaneous	12,274	1,023	0.51	$429,590
Total Gold Returned by U.S.	**7,625,305**		**317.72**	**$266,885,675**
Balance On Hand June 1950	**2,461,114**	**205,093**	**102.55**	**$86,138,990**
Balance on Hand - 1995 Value				$984,445,600

Notes

I n an attempt to make this study as readable as possible, I have not footnoted every fact and assertion. These note, however, do list the main records and publications upon which I relied. I have in my possession a copy of all source documents used in the writing of this book, and encourage interested parties with any additional information about these items or other to write me: Kenneth D. Alford, P. O. Box 3694, Richmond, VA 23235. You may also e-mail me at: kalford@compuserve.com.

Abbreviations

CMH	U.S. Army Center of Military History, Washington D.C.
JAG	U.S. Army Judiciary, Falls Church, Virginia
LC	Library of Congress, Manuscript Division, Washington, D.C.
MHI	U.S. Army Military History Institute, Carlisle Barracks, PA
NGA	National Gallery of Art, Washington D.C.
NA	National Archives, College Park, Maryland
RG	Record Group

Chapter 1: The Allied Capture of Nazi Gold

NA, RG260/420-441, The Records of the Foreign Exchange Depository contains the bulk of the firsthand documentation relied on for this chapter.

1. CMH, "G-4 Functions in ETOUSA Operations", April 9 to April 22, 1945.
2. Bernard Bernstein: Taped interview, May 19, 1984
3. Bernard Bernstein: Taped interview, May 19, 1984
4. Bernard Bernstein: Taped interview, May 19, 1984.
5. General George Patton, *War as I Knew It,* 1947.
6. Bernard Bernstein, Telephone interview, July 1986.
7. Bernard Bernstein, Taped interview, May 19, 1984.
8. Bernard Bernstein, Taped interview, May 19, 1984.
9. NA, RG 332, L.F. Murray, "Report of Alleged Discrepancies in Currency and Coin Found in Mine at Merkers, Germany, May 7, 1945."
10. NA, RG260, Ardelia Hall Collection

Chapter 2: The Plundering of Munich

1. NA, RG 332, Testimony of Captain Paul M. Leake, July 31, 1945.
2. NA, RG 332, "Report of Investigation Regarding Certain Silverware Mailed Home By Private First Class Theodore J. Polski to His Wife Mrs. Grace Polski, September 7, 1945."

Chapter 3: Hermann Göring's Art Treasure

1. NGA, S. Lane Fason Papers, OSS Consolidation Interrogation Report No. 2
2. NA, RG260/439, Taper and Breitenbach, Report on Field Trip to Berchtesgaden.
3. Thomas M. Johnson, *World War II German War Booty, Volume II*, pp. 45-47.

Chapter 4: The Capture of Hermann Göring

1. NA, RG332, Joseph M. Whitaker: Fraternization by General Officers of 36th Division, May 22, 1945.
2. NA, RG 332, Arthur A. White: Letter to Inspector General, May 21, 1947.
3. NA, RG338, Records of the Seventh Army Interrogation Center.
4. NA, RG260, H.K. Röthel, MFA&A Section, Interrogation of Robert Kropp, March 26, 1947.
5. NA, RG260, Ardelia Hall Collection, Interrogation by Herbert S. Leonard, August 31, 1946.

6. Thomas M. Johnson, *Collecting the Edged Weapons of the Third Reich*, Volume VIII, pp. 88-105.

7. NA, RG260, Ardelia Hall Collection, Paul R. Eaton, Criminal Investigation Report, December 16, 1947.

8. MHI, William W. Quinn, "Correspondence and Court-Martial of Major Paul Kubala."

9. Jason Benjamin, ANWPM 201-KUBUALA , Paul A. Off -Headquarters Military District of Washington, Room 5-B-518, The Pentagon, March 5, 1948.

Chapter 5: The Looting of Berchtesgaden

1. Harry Sions, *Yank*, April 1945.

2. NA, RG 165, Civil Affairs Division, Graham W. Lester, "Investigation concerning removal from Germany of Field Marshal Goering's medallion and baton, June 16, 1947."

3. Austin History Center, July 1945, unidentifed newspaper clipping.

4. Thomas M. Johnson, *World War II German War Booty*, Volume II, p. 27

5. Bernard Bernstein: Interview, December 1986.

Chapter 6: Sepp Dietrich's Souvenirs

1. Thomas M. Johnson, *World War II German War Booty*, Volume II, pp. 14-17.

Chapter 7: The Military Governor of Weimar

JAG, Court-Martial Lieutenant Colonel William M. Brown, February 1946. The material used for this chapter was taken primarily from Brown's 600 page courts-martial record.

1. JAG, Hans Muller, Testimony, June 29, 1945.

2. JAG, Gustav Giesel statement to the Weimar Criminal Police Station, June 13, 1945.

3. JAG, John Vogler, Testimony, June 27, 1945.

4. JAG, William M. Brown, Sworn Statement to Assistant Inspector General, Arthur V. Patterson, June 27, 1945.

5. NA, RG 59, Ardelia Hall Collection, Paul Estes, Oral Statement to Marvin T. Farmer, July 21, 1954.

6. *New York Times*, May 1, 1966.

7. NA, RG 59/4, Ardelia Hall Collection.

Chapter 8: The Buried Treasure of Buchenwald

1. NA, RG260/420-441, Records of the Foreign Exchange Depository.
2. NA, RG260/7-12, U.S. Forces Austria.

Chapter 9: Operation Macabre

1. NA, RG260, Ardelia Hall Collection, Walter Hancock's MFA&A Report, May 12, 1945.
2. Walter Hancock, A Monuments Officer in Germany, *College Art Journal*, May 1946.
3. Will Lang: "The Case of the Distinguished Corpses," *Life Magazine*, 1948.
4. NA, RG260, Captain M.G. Karsner, *Shrines to Executed Nazis*, January 6, 1947.

Chapter 10: The Collection Points

1. NA, RG260/777-780, Records of Museums, Fine arts, and Archives Section.
2. LC, The European Mission & Cooperative Acquisition Project/34, Offenbach Archival Depot.
3. NA, RG260/250-262, Ardelia Hall Collection, L. Wilkins, "Material Wrongfully sent from Offenbach and Presently in Jerusalem, May 27, 1947."
4. NA, RG260/250-262, Ardelia Hall Collection, Memorandum of Agreement, February 15, 1949.
5. NA, RG260/51-232, Ardelia Hall Collection.
6. NGA, The Edith Standen Papers.
7. NA, RG260/263-550, Ardelia Hall Collection.
8. NGA, The Edith Standen Papers.
9. NGA, The Edward E. Adams Papers.

Chapter 11: The Imperial Crown Jewels of the Holy Roman Empire

1. NA, RG260/1, U.S. Forces Austria, Records of Monuments and Fine Art Branch, "Crown Jewels of the Holy Roman Empire."
2. NA, RG260/34, Ardelia Hall Collection, Horns Report, August 14, 1945.
3. CMH, Alton C. Miller, Investigation of Alleged Grand Larceny, September 1946.
4. NGA, Everett P. Lesley Paper.

Chapter 12: Saint Stephen's Crown

Department of State, Freedom of Information Request 9104455.
1. Paul Kubala, Written Statement, August 2,1945.
2. Otto V. Falke, "The Crown of St. Stephen," undated.
3. *Hungarian Weekly*, Munich, July 7, 1950.

Chapter 13: The Theft of the Hesse Crown Jewels

1. JAG, Court-Martials, Captain Kathleen Nash, Major David Watson and Colonel Jack Durant, 1946.
2. Kenneth D. Alford, *The Spoils of World War II*, New York 1994.

Chapter 14: German War Art

1. CMH, Gordon W. Gilkey: Report, "German War Art."

Chapter 15: The Pillage of the Fabulous Horses of Europe

1. NA, RG260.
2. Gordon W. Cook: "Equine Reparations," *The Quartermaster Review,* September-October, 1946.
3. Daniel P. Mannix: "The Superhorses Are Ours," *Collier's,* August 17, 1946.

Chapter 16: The Return of the Hersbruck Soldiers

1. NA, RG 59/8, Ardelia Hall Collection. Hersbruck 50,000 Tin Soldiers.

Chapter 17: The Heinrich Hoffmann Photograph Collection

1. NA, RG226/15, Putzi Hanfstaengl: Statement to OSS, August 31, 1942.
2. NA, RG338/2632, EUCOM Historical Division.
3. NA, Nontextual Archives Division, Elizabeth L. Hill's working file.

Chapter 18: Theft of the Quedlinburg Church Treasure

1. *New York Times,* June 14, 1990.
2. NA, RG 260, "Art Looting By American Personnel (ALBAP)."

3. General Courts-Martial, Meador, Joe T.; November 17, 1945.

4. *The Washington Post*, July 11, 1990.

5. Author's participation and interviews with Willi Korte during this quest.

Chapter 19: Adolf Eichmann's Treasure Map

1. NA, RG338, NND 836507, unnumbered box, Screened George C. Chalou, 7/18/83.

Chapter 20: The Mystery of the Missing Amber Room

1. Dr. Klaus Goldmann: "The Deposits in the Steinsalzbergwerk Braunschweig - Lüneburg in Grasleben," Berlin, November, 1987.

2. Author's Telephone Interview with Lamont Moore, late 1980s.

3. NA, RG 153, *U.S. v. Andrae et al.* (Dora).

4. Paul Enke, Bernstein Zimmer Report, June 30, 1986, Berlin Germany.

5. Wolfgang Schneider, Documentation of the Whereabouts of the Amber Room, September 24, 1992; NA, RG 153/270-273, *U.S. v. Andrae et al.*

Chapter 21: The Library of Congress Mission

The Library of Congress documents are from The European Mission & Cooperative Acquisition Project, boxes 1 through 36.

1. LC, Reuben Peiss: European Wartime Acquisitions and Library of Congress Mission, undated.

2. LC, Don C. Travis: Letter to Mortimer Traube, Library of Congress Mission, May 26, 1947.

3. LC, Joseph Groesbech: Letter to Mr. Frederick Goff, Library of Congress, July 1, 1952.

4. NA, RG 331/18, Target List and Reports of Target Teams.

Bibliography

The source material used to prepare this study was largely obtained from manuscript documents, which are listed under the notes for each specific chapter and entry. The titles listed below were also used, largely for general background information.

Published Sources

Alford, Kenneth D. *The Spoils of World War II*. New York: Birch Lane Press, 1994.

Botting, Douglas. *The Aftermath: Europe*. Virginia: Time-Life, 1982.

Bradley,Omar N. *A Soldier's Story*. New York: Henry Hold & Company, 1951.

——, A General's Life. New York: Simon & Schuster, 1983.

Eisenhower, Dwight D. *Crusade in Europe*. New York: Doubleday & Co., 1948.

Hoehne, Heinz. *The Order of the Death's Head*. New York: Ballantine Books, 1969.

Howe, Thomas Carr Jr. *Salt Mines and Castles*. New York: Bobbs-Merrill Co., 1946.

Irving, David. *Göring*. New York: William Morrow and Company, Inc., 1989.

Johnson, Thomas M. *World War II German War Booty*. Columbia, South Carolina: Published privately by the author, 1984.

——, *World War II German War Booty* Volume II: Columbia, South Carolina: Published privately by the author, 1984.

230

MacDonald, Charles B. *The Last Offensive.* Washington D.C.: U.S. Government Printing Office, 1984.

Nicholas, Lynn H. *The Rape of Europa.* New York: Alfred A. Knopf, 1994.

Patton, George C. *War As I Knew It.* Boston: Houghton Mifflin Co., 1947.

Ryan, Cornelus. *The Last Battle.* New York: Simon & Schuster, 1966.

Schellenberg, Walter. *The Labyrinth.* New York: Harper & Brothers, 1956.

Shirer, William L. *The Rise and Fall of The Third Reich.* New York: Simon and Schuster, 1960.

Stanley-Moss W. *Gold is Where You Hide It.* London: 1968.

Toland, John. *The Last 100 Days.* New York: Random House, 1965.

——, *Adolf Hitler.* New York: Doubleday, 1976.

Trevor-Roper, Hugh R. *The Last Days of Hitler.* London: The Macmillan Company, 1947.

U.S. Department of State. *Foreign Relations of the United States,* Volumes for 1944-1946. Washington, D.C.: U.S. Government Printing Office, 1955.

Ziemke, Earl F., *The U.S. Army in the Occupation of Germany.* Washington D.C.: U.S. Government Printing Office, 1975.

INDEX